Making Jewellery with Gemstone Beads

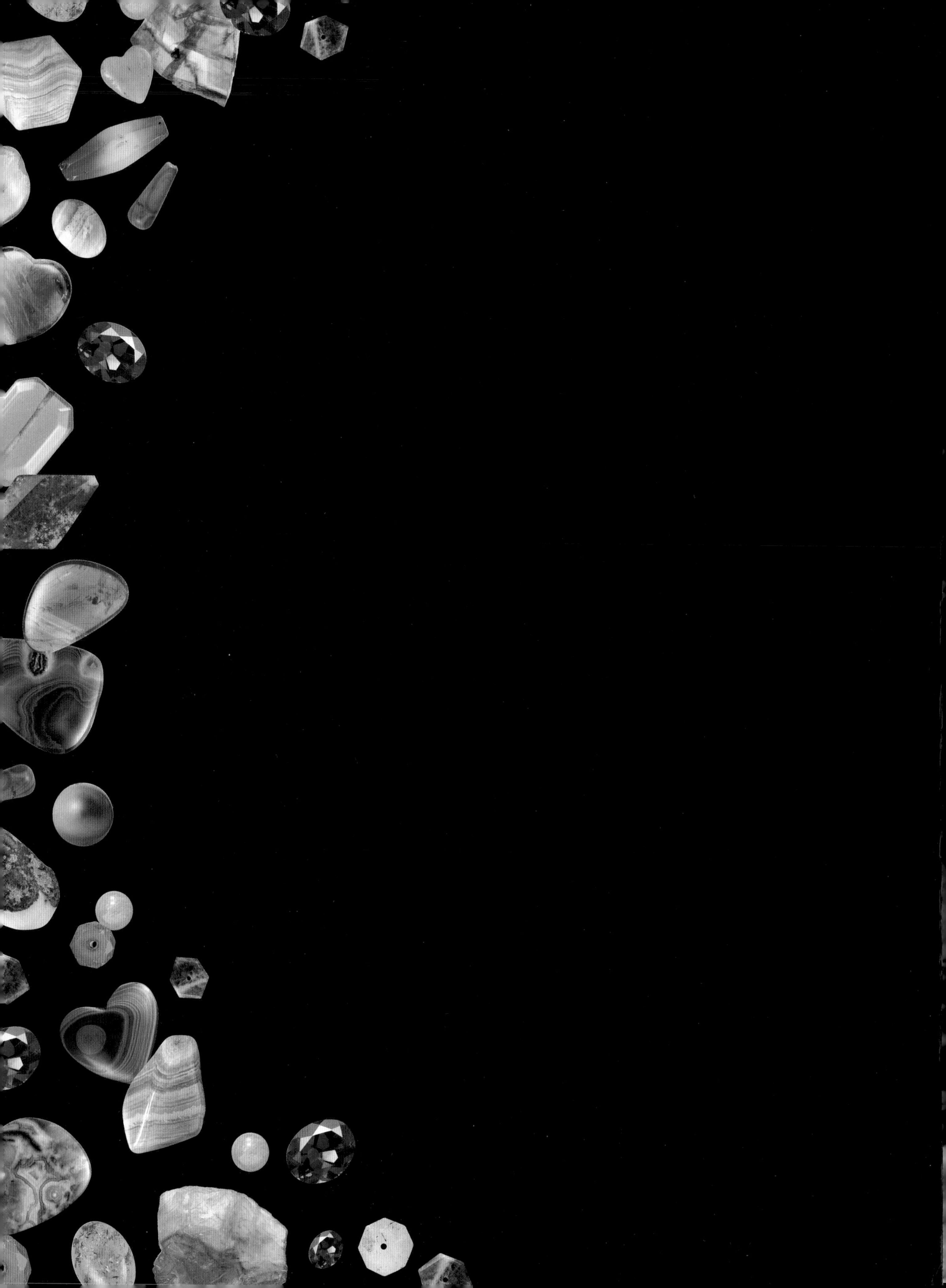

Making Jewellery with Gemstone Beads

Barbara Case

A DAVID & CHARLES BOOK

David & Charles is an F+W Publications Inc. company
4700 East Galbraith Road
Cincinnati, OH 45236

First published in the UK in 2007

A catalogue record for this book is available from the British Library.

ISBN-13: 978-0-7153-2594-0 paperback
ISBN-10: 0-7153-2594-9 paperback

Printed in China by SNP Leefung Pte Ltd
for David & Charles
Brunel House Newton Abbot Devon

Commissioning Editor Vivienne Wells
Desk Editor Bethany Dymond
Head of Design Prudence Rogers
Art Editor Sarah Underhill
Senior Designer Charly Bailey
Designer Alistair Barnes
Project Editor Jo Richardson
Production Controller Ros Napper
Photographer Paul Biddle

Visit our website at www.davidandcharles.co.uk

David & Charles books are available from all good bookshops; alternatively, you can contact our Orderline on 0870 9908222 or write to us at FREEPOST EX2 110, D&C Direct, Newton Abbot, TQ12 4ZZ (no stamp required UK only); US customers call 800-289-0963 and Canadian customers call 800-840-5220.

Contents

Introduction

Making beaded jewellery with the wonderful range of natural stone that our world has to offer takes us back to basics, because in the early days of our history, naturally occurring 'beads' such as shells or stones formed with holes were all we had to create with.

Today, sophisticated tools and modern mining methods have brought the minerals and crystals found beneath our feet within our grasp, to give us a truly fabulous choice of natural stone beads in an array of colours that vie with those produced by skilled glass bead makers. The raw material for these beads was formed millennia ago in deep underground areas, where the Earth's evolution turned them into something special – the wonderful coloured stones that attract us so much now. Over vast periods of time, the Earth's constant yet slow movement and the action of water have, in some instances, brought these substances to the surface; hence the occasional, but incredibly fortunate, find of precious stones such as sapphires or diamonds in river beds. However, for most of us, beads made from these rare treasure troves are an infrequent sight, although we do have a huge and, it seems, ever-increasing variety of natural stone beads from which to choose.

Most people refer to diamonds, sapphires, rubies and emeralds as 'precious stones' while amethyst, citrine, aquamarine, topaz and the like are known as 'semi-precious stones.' Then there are the so-called 'ornamental stones,' such as jasper, obsidian, agate and aventurine. But they are all natural stones, so when I use the term 'natural stones' or 'stones,' please don't confuse these with the comparatively uninteresting-looking everyday stone or pebble found in soil or on sandy shores, and bear in mind that the most exotic item of all, the diamond, is also frequently referred to simply as a 'stone.'

So, natural stones can be found in almost any imaginable colour, and some are opaque, some transparent and others crystal clear. Some appear in bands of contrasting colour, while others have mottled or flecked colours. Yet more change colour in certain lights and several stones appear in such a variety of colours that the inexperienced could easily believe each colour to be an entirely different stone.

To me, the joy of working with natural stone beads is their variety and their sense of age. Consider, as you hold them in your hand and observe their beauty, that their actual substance was provided by the ground beneath you in a process that began millions of years before man was in his infancy.

Almost all corners of the world offer some type of ornamental stone, with a few places being world famous for particular stones, such as Sri Lanka for its sapphires, Africa for its diamonds and Afghanistan for its lapis lazuli. In the UK, the Scottish mountains yield up a few rare Cairngorms, while Derbyshire is known for its blue John (a variety of fluorite) and Whitby for its jet. Today, as I write, the newspapers hold reports of an African find of the largest diamond ever, about two-thirds the size of a cricket ball!

Long before modern-day beading, people had a fascination with beautiful artefacts, and chance finds of coloured stones stirred their imagination so that they kept these items about them and, where possible, fashioned them into adornments. Thus we have had such a long association with many of these stones that they have become entwined in folklore and legend, handed down from generation to generation. It also seems that for as long as we have prized these treasures for their beauty, we have also held a belief in their powers – for example, no witch doctor of repute would have been considered 'worth his salt' if his 'kit' hadn't contained the right stones!

Within these pages I bring you a wide variety of stone types, tell some of their lore, legend and history, present some gorgeous photographs and offer as wide a range of jewellery projects as my imagination will allow. Many projects combine other types of bead, such as glass and metal, with the natural stones, and sometimes I mix stone types together. However, there are no rules, and if you wish you can make up the designs in any beads of your choice.

Last of all, don't make the mistake of believing that beads made from natural materials are for the wealthy only, as many projects within the book are less expensive than if they had been made with purely man-made beads such as glass or metal!

About this book

The front section offers a comprehensive guide to natural stone beads and their threading materials, concise advice on the tools and equipment you need, together with clear instructions on the basic techniques involved in the projects. Each subsequent section focuses on a natural stone from which the beads featured in the accompanying projects are made. Each project is set out in 'recipe' style, with an 'ingredients' list, followed by a step-by-step 'method'. While the ingredients lists are detailed, don't feel restricted by my choices. Look at each project and consider the alterations that you could make to adapt it to your own tastes – you may prefer a different colour or length, a slight variation in the design or to use beads other than those shown. However, when you first start, pick a few simple projects to follow exactly before you progress to make your own versions. To help you decide which projects you are ready for, I have graded them on a scale of 1–10, with 1 being the simplest and 10 the most complex. I also give an approximate length of time that a beginner might expect to take to make each item.

Most natural stone beads are supplied loose strung, i.e. temporarily strung, usually in lengths of 40cm (16in). This is the least expensive way to purchase them and you should not be put off, even if you want only a few beads, as there are lots of ways in which you can use any leftovers.

Materials

In general, the materials needed for making jewellery with gemstone beads are no different from those required for any other type of bead. However, when using expensive beads of any kind, I believe that it is best to use other components to match, so most projects in the book include metal beads and findings that are made from sterling silver, goldfill, high-quality silver or gold plate, or anodized niobium.

Beads

As you know, this book focuses on beads made from natural stone, but remember that this encompasses all types of natural stone, including precious, semi-precious and ornamental. Other beads have also been used in the projects in conjunction with these natural stone beads in order to enhance them, add variety, match colours and reduce cost. For the most part, these additional items are metal, but I have also used glass beads, usually rocailles, but a few coloured glass crystal beads have found their way into some projects.

For those daunted by the prospect of finding the beads shown, don't worry! Natural stone beads are more popular today than ever before, and a vast variety of bead types in a multitude of shapes and sizes is available to the everyday beader from most bead suppliers. It is also possible to make any of these projects in other types of bead. So, as in my previous books, I hope that you will use my ideas as a springboard for your own imagination.

As you look through the pages of the book, you will realize that natural stone beads are to be found in a huge range of colours, from subtle shades to brilliant hues, and, depending on the stone type, in many sizes, too. The raw material for some stones, such as peridot and emerald, doesn't lend itself to big beads, but others, such as agate, carnelian and jasper, are formed in large masses, which means that they can be made into large beads and elaborate shapes.

The most common shapes of bead, such as round, faceted, tumble-chip and baroque, are normally easily available at all times. However, when purchasing natural stone beads of unusual shape, you should be aware that supply may not always be continuous. This is because there are few bead makers who produce these special beads and they do so from a limited stock of what they have to hand. Therefore, when they run out of a particular raw material, they will switch to producing a different type of bead. So, if you find a type of bead you love and you know that you will want more, it is worth purchasing larger quantities than you require for your immediate needs.

The chart on pages 10–11 itemizes the main types of natural stone bead seen within the book and their key details, such as size, shape, cost and attributes. Each chapter gives you additional information about the beads used, and I hope that as you progress through the book, you will come to share some of my own joy in using beads that are formed from the very fabric of our world.

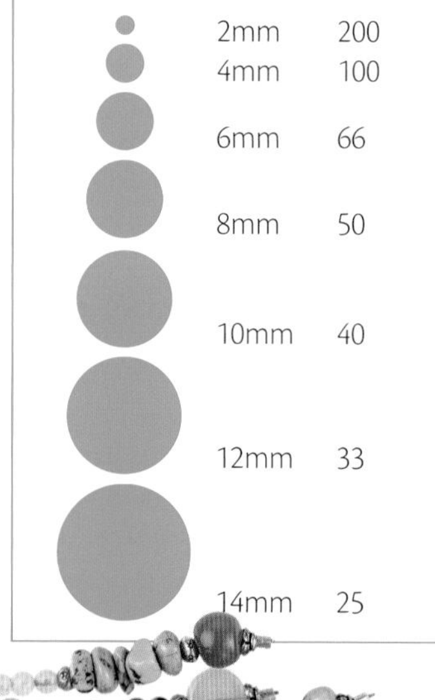

Safety Note
Beads are relatively small items and should therefore be kept out of the reach of very young children. It is also advisable to supervise older children when jewellery making until they become competent at handling the tools and sharp materials, such as wire.

Threading Materials

Because semi-precious stone beads are made by different methods to most other beads – that is, the holes are drilled – the edges are often relatively sharp. Therefore, to make sure that my necklaces are supple yet strong, I have used nylon-coated wire for most of the threading. This wire is an incredibly strong version of the old, stiff tiger-tail. Its suppleness is afforded by up to 49 tiny strands of wire beneath a flexible coating of nylon. I know of only two manufacturers producing this wire: Softflex and Beadalon. It is available in various diameters, which for simplicity I describe as fine, medium and thick, and a wide range of colours, but in practice the colour is usually unimportant, as the wire is hidden beneath the beads and gimp.

There are many types of beading thread to choose from, varying from synthetic to real silk (the latter often comes ready-threaded with a flexible needle), and most are available in a wide range of colours. I use beading thread in two situations: when the beads are very lightweight, and when I want the thread to show, as in knotting when the thread becomes an integral part of the design. Other main materials used for threading are waxed cotton cord, faux suede (available in a wide range of colours) and memory wire (a springy wire that 'remembers' its shape). All of these and any others not mentioned here are discussed in more detail within the chapter where they are used.

Gimp, Crimp Beads and Calottes

These items are the means by which your 'thread' is attached to the clasp to ensure a neat, attractive and strong fixing. Gimp is a length of extremely fine, coiled wire that is used in conjunction with crimp beads or in a knotted necklace to cover the 'thread' where it attaches to the clasp. Usually silver- or gold-coloured gimp is satisfactory, but occasionally coloured gimp can be useful, as it can be matched to the beads.

Crimp beads are small, soft metal beads that are used in conjunction with nylon-coated wire to form loops that attach the wire to the clasp.

Calottes are metal findings made in various shapes that close (with the aid of pliers) over the end of the 'thread' to provide a strong fixing point to the clasp. There are several ways of using calottes and these are demonstrated under Basic Necklace Stringing, pages 14–16, and in the individual projects.

Findings

These are the metal connecting pieces, such as clasps, headpins and ear-hooks, that make your jewellery work. You will note that the majority of projects are made with gold findings and beads, but this is not necessarily preferable and you can always use silver. My choice was based purely on practicality – in writing this book, I made projects way ahead of photography, and when left unworn, silver tarnishes, so just imagine all that cleaning of intricate beads and clasps a year after making the items!

Nickel Allergy

Many people will be aware that nickel, sometimes used in the manufacture of findings, can cause allergic reactions. In recent times, the EU consequently brought in a directive to reduce the amount permitted to minute proportions and disallowed the sale of jewellery containing higher nickel content. However, not all countries adhere to these restrictions, and in the USA, for instance, nickel is still used in some jewellery metals. If this issue affects you and you purchase products made in a non-EU country, you should check the nickel status for yourself before purchasing.

STONE TYPE	ROUND – SIZE	OTHER SHAPES	COST	BIRTHSTONE	ATTRIBUTES REPUTEDLY CONFERRED OR AIDED
agate (general)	4–12mm	✓	low	Gemini	longevity, protection
amazonite	4–8mm	✓	low	Virgo	new beginnings – stabilizing, soothing
amber	4–20mm	✓	medium–very high	Leo	healing, beauty
amethyst	2–16mm	✓	low–medium	Aquarius, Pisces, Sagittarius	protection, romance
ametrine	6–8mm	✓	medium–high	Aquarius, Libra, Scorpio	compatibility, relief from stress
aquamarine	2–6mm	✓	low–very high	Aquarius, Pisces, Taurus	inspiration, healing, self-knowledge
aventurine	4–10mm	✓	low	Gemini, Virgo	prosperity, leadership
azurite	4–12mm	✓	medium	Sagittarius	meditation, fights arthritis & helps joints
bloodstone	3–10mm	✓	low	Pisces, Sagittarius	combats depression and infection, vitality
blue lace agate	3–12mm	✓	low	Gemini, Taurus	calming, cooling, good for infections
Botswana agate	4–12mm	✓	low	Gemini, Taurus	self-confidence, balancing, healing
calcite (various colours)	6–20mm	✓	low		comforting, cheering, intuition
carnelian agate	3–10mm	✓	low	Leo, Virgo	healing, protecting, good health
chrysoprase	4–10mm		low–high	Libra	fertility, light-heartedness
chrysotile	4–10mm	✓	low	Taurus	bonding, integrity
citrine/smoky quartz	4–8mm	✓	low–medium	Libra, Scorpio	self-worth, prosperity
crazy lace agate	4–10mm	✓	low		security, healing
diamond	Not in bead form		very high	Taurus	purity, energy
emerald	2–6mm	✓	very high	Taurus, Cancer	memory, eloquence, forward vision
fluorite (various colours)	3–20mm	✓	low	Pisces, Capricorn	physical perfection, analytical ability
garnet	2–8mm	✓	medium	Capricorn, Aries	endurance, confidence, attracts love
hematite/hematine	3–12mm	✓	very low	Aquarius	stress, memory, positive thinking
howlite	4–10mm	✓	very low	Gemini	communication
iolite	4–5mm	✓	low–medium	Aquarius, Taurus	understanding, expression

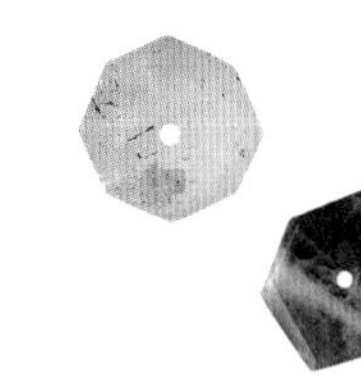

STONE TYPE	ROUND – SIZE	OTHER SHAPES	COST	BIRTHSTONE	ATTRIBUTES REPUTEDLY CONFERRED OR AIDED
jade (various types)	4–12mm	✓	low–high	Taurus	protection on journeys, luck
jasper (various types)	4–12mm	✓	low	Pisces	stabilizing, protecting
labradorite	4–12mm	✓	low–high	Scorpio	awareness, attunement
lapis lazuli	3–12mm	✓	medium–high	Sagittarius, Taurus, Libra	wisdom, truth, awareness
malachite	3–10mm	✓	medium	Capricorn, Scorpio	happiness, hope, health, security
moldovite	no beads		high		healing, transforming
moonstone	4–8mm	✓	low–high	Cancer	safety at sea, fruitful crops
moss agate	3–10mm	✓	low	Virgo	emotional equilibrium
obsidian – mahogany and snowflake	4–10mm	✓	low		grounding, purification, fulfilment
onyx (various colours)	3–15mm		low	Cancer, Leo	concentration, devotion
opal	4–6mm	✓	medium–very high	Libra	psychic ability, love
pearl	3–10mm	✓	medium	Gemini	purity, simplicity
peridot	3–5mm	✓	medium	Leo, Libra	protective, calming
rhodocrosite	4–10mm	✓	low–medium	Scorpio, Leo	love, balancing
rock crystal/quartz	3–20mm	✓	low	Taurus	protection, intuition, mysticism
rose quartz	3–20mm	✓	low	Virgo	friendship and love
ruby	3–5mm	✓	very high	Capricorn, Cancer	creativity, gentleness, monetary gain
sapphire	3–5mm	✓	very high	Taurus, Gemini	kindness, sincerity
sodalite	3–10mm	✓	low	Sagittarius	logical thinking, truth
tiger eye	3–10mm	✓	low	Capricorn	courage, self-confidence, clear thinking
topaz	4–5mm		low–high	Taurus, Scorpio	health, stress, calming
tourmaline	3–5mm	✓	medium–high	Pisces, Libra, Gemini, Cancer	protective, inspirational
turquoise	4–10mm	✓	low–high	Sagittarius	protective, good fortune, wealth
zoisite	4–8mm		low–medium		fertility

Tools & Equipment

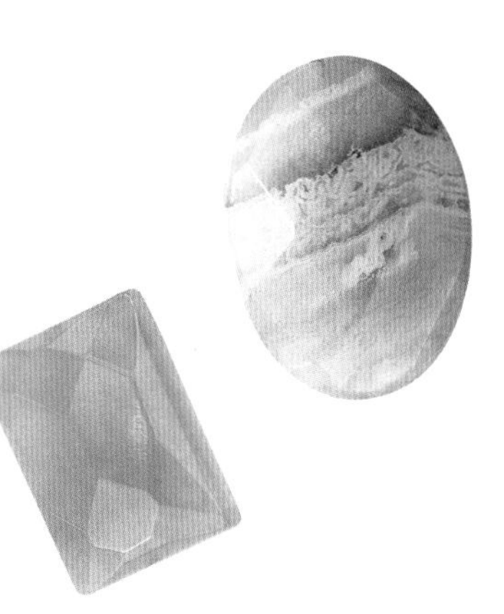

It is not necessary to purchase lots of expensive equipment to start making beaded jewellery, and all the prospective beader needs are the few items listed in the Basic Tool Kit below. However, in due course you are likely to become engrossed in the hobby and then wish to seek out the more specialist tools mentioned here. There is no doubt that using the right equipment will make things much easier for you!

Basic Tool Kit

For each project, you will require the following items; only additional specialist tools are itemized in the individual ingredients lists where needed.

- pair of cutting, round and flat-nosed pliers, or a small pair of general-purpose beading pliers (see right)
- sharp pair of scissors
- beading tray or household tray with separate shallow containers

Pliers

Having the appropriate pliers is essential if you are to make a lot of jewellery. They come in a variety of types that are each suited to their own job. Bead suppliers sell most types of pliers in a range of qualities, and as the old saying goes, you get what you pay for. Germany produces the best and most expensive pliers, and if you take the plunge and purchase these, they should last a lifetime. However, pliers at less than a third of the price are perfectly suited to the job, even if they are less durable.

General-purpose Beading Pliers

If you are restricted by cost to just one type of pliers, these are the ones to go for. They do all the jobs that most of the other pliers are designed to do, but without quite the same degree of ease.

Round-nosed Pliers

If you intend to make significant quantities of earrings, then you should purchase these, as they make the task of forming loops in wire/headpins so much easier.

Cutting Pliers

Although general-purpose pliers provide a cutting facility, they are best suited to cutting easily accessible wire. When it comes to cutting wire in an area with restricted access, cutting pliers are invaluable.

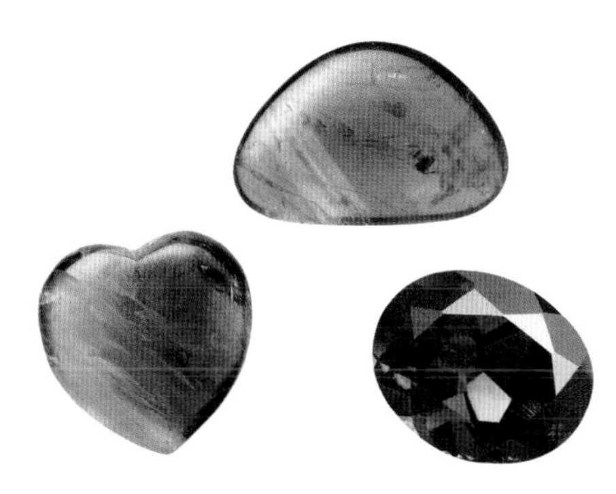

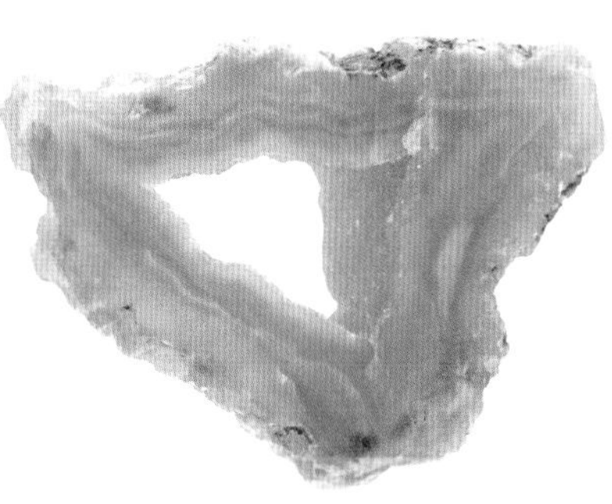

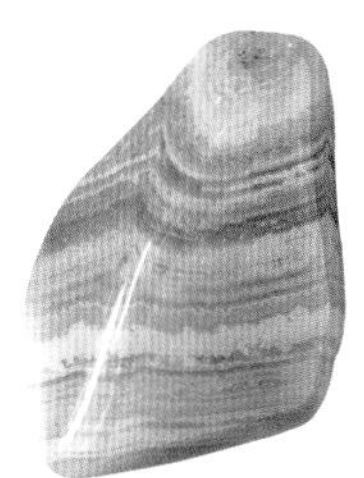

Crimp Pliers

Crimp pliers are a relatively recent innovation designed specifically for use with high-quality crimp beads and nylon-coated wire. They are used to secure the wire onto a clasp with a very neat finish. Without the use of crimp pliers, the beader only has the option of squeezing a crimp bead onto wire with a pair of general-purpose pliers, and this produces a flat crimp rather than a rounded one.

Storage Containers

All beaders need them! However, the type you choose is purely a matter of personal preference and available space. Among those on offer are mini chests of drawers, portable compartmentalized plastic 'suitcases', little plastic tubes and carousels. Take a look at a supplier's catalogue or visit a DIY store and choose what suits you best. If you decide to do a lot of work with natural stones, it might be worth investing in a necklace stand, as this allows you to hang many strings of loose beads in a small area and also enables you to see at a glance what you have to hand.

Beading Trays

There are many types of beading tray available and all are designed to hold your beads while you are making jewellery. I find the most useful are those with grooves in which you can lay the beads in the proposed order of threading, as this provides for swapping them around within a design before they are actually committed to a string. There is no doubt that you can easily work at beading using a domestic tray and several small, flat containers to hold your beads, and in some ways this can be preferable to using a purpose-built tray, which offers less space. I also find that small, flat containers are easier when it comes to picking up small beads from them, as well as emptying them when finished with the beads.

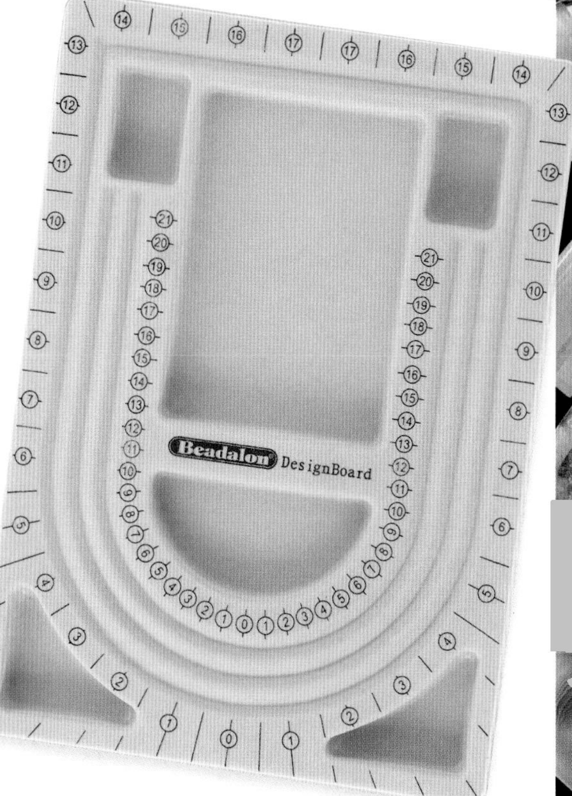

Bead Reamer

For anyone working frequently with semi-precious stone, a bead reamer is almost essential, as it saves the frustration of discarding the last bead of a string that resolutely refuses to be strung because its hole is too small! The tool is a hand-held tube in which are stored three different sizes and shapes of round file. At one end of the tube is a small chuck, into which the required file is fitted, to enable the enlargement of most bead holes with minimal effort. Eventually this tool will pay for itself in salvaged beads.

Basic Techniques

Most of the routine techniques used in the projects are explained here. If you can master even just a few of these easy techniques, you will have acquired the skills needed to string a simple necklace and make a pair of earrings.

Basic Necklace Stringing

The following techniques show how to attach various threading mediums to necklace clasps. There are various ways of doing this for each type of thread or wire, so I have presented them in order of most frequent use within the book. More specialist techniques are covered within the projects where they are used.

TIP
Before starting to thread a necklace, assemble all your ingredients on a purpose-made beading tray or a household tray with separate shallow containers.

All semi-precious stone beads are handmade and this can mean that they are not uniform in size. Look carefully at your beads and make sure that you use the different sizes accordingly, i.e. in most designs the larger beads should be kept for the front of the necklace, with the smaller ones positioned close to the clasp.

Using Nylon-coated Wire with Crimp Beads

1 Thread a crimp bead onto one end of the wire, then thread the wire through the loop of one part of a clasp. Thread the wire back through the crimp bead to make a small loop (diagram A).

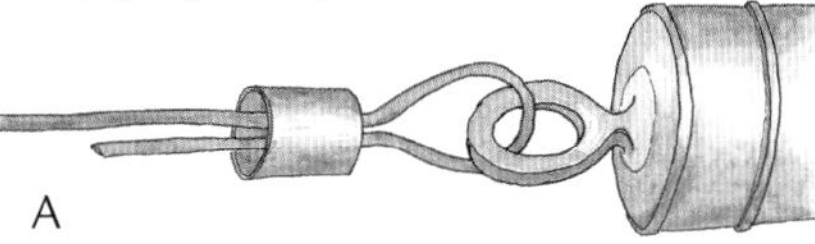

2 Use pliers to close the crimp bead to secure it to the wire – see diagrams B and C for using general-purpose beading pliers and diagrams D–F for using specialist crimp pliers.

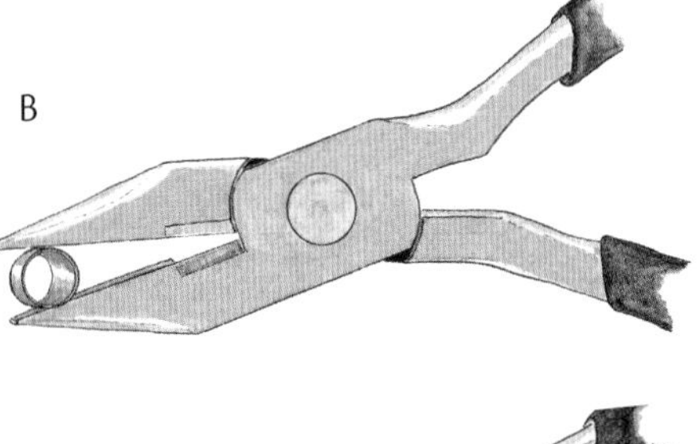

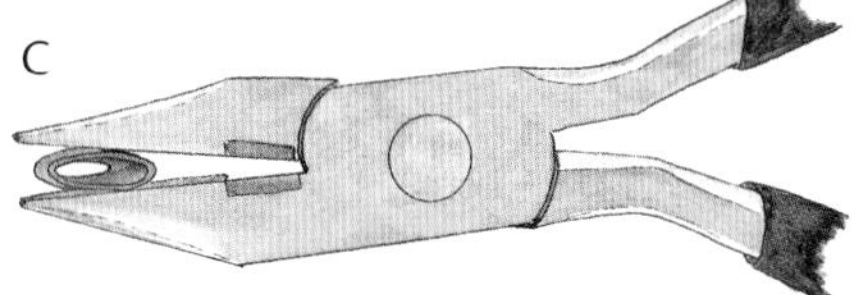

Using specialist crimp pliers is a two-part process, as there are two sets of grooves in its 'jaws'. First, place the crimp bead into groove 'a' and squeeze. Then place it into groove 'b' and squeeze the pliers again to round the crimp (diagrams D–F). The diagrams are shown in profile and without the nylon-coated wire for extra clarity.

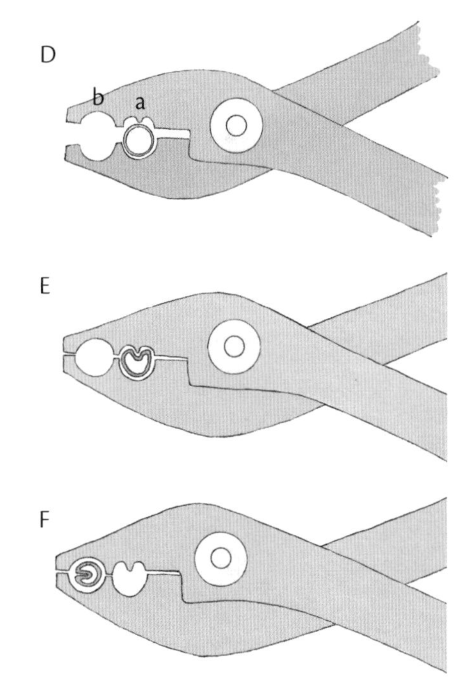

3 After securing the crimp bead, use cutting pliers to trim the spare wire close to the crimp bead (diagram G).

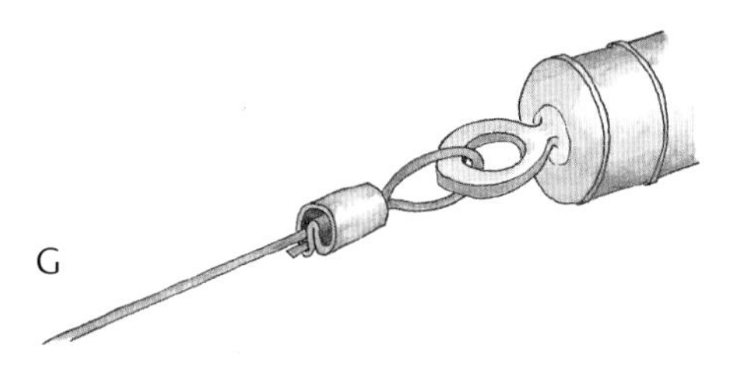

Using Nylon-coated Wire with Gimp and Crimp Beads

The technique is exactly as opposite, but instead of leaving the wire loop bare, it is covered by gimp for a more attractive and professional finish. With a pair of cutting pliers, cut an 8mm (⅜in) length of gimp, then follow the instructions opposite, but after threading on the crimp bead, thread on the length of gimp to cover the wire (diagrams A and B).

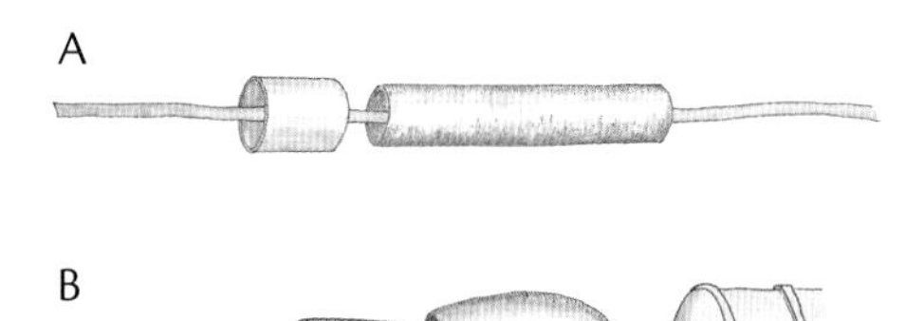

Using Nylon-coated Wire with Crimp Beads and Clamshell Calottes

1 Apply a crimp bead to the end of a length of nylon-coated wire and squeeze it firmly in place. Thread the wire through the hole of a clamshell calotte and pull so that the crimp bead sits inside the 'shell' of the calotte (diagram A).

2 Use cutting pliers to trim the spare wire and then use general-purpose pliers to close the calotte. Use the same pliers to open the loop of the calotte and attach it to the clasp, and again to close the loop (diagram B).

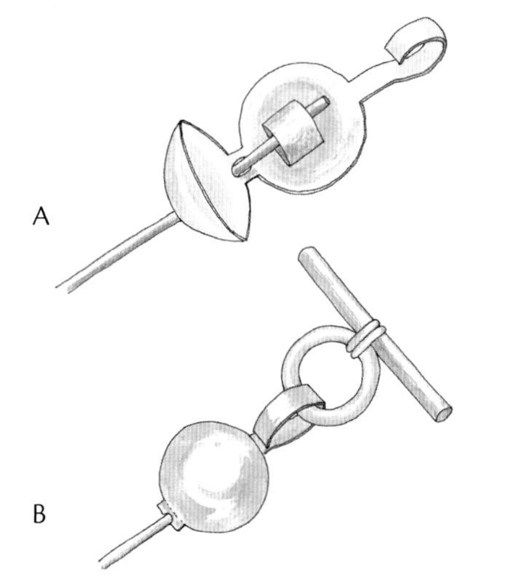

Using Beading Thread with Gimp

1 Thread an 8mm (⅜in) length of gimp onto beading thread, then thread on the loop of the clasp. Use the short end of the thread to tie an overhand knot around the thread at the other end of the gimp (diagram A).

2 Pull the knot tight, then use a headpin to apply a tiny touch of superglue to the knot to seal it. Trim any spare thread. Do not get superglue on your beads!

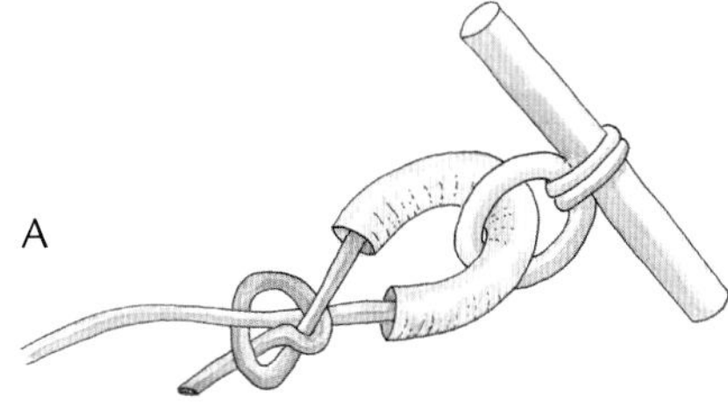

Using Beading Thread with Clamshell Calottes

This technique is ideal for beginners and those who are unsure about making neat knots. It can also be used with cord, but you will need to use a larger-sized calotte.

1 Tie a double overhand knot in a length of beading thread, or alternatively tie on a small rocaille bead (diagrams A and B).

2 Use a headpin to apply a tiny touch of superglue to the knot, then trim any spare thread. Thread the beading thread through the hole of a clamshell calotte and pull so that the knot (or bead) sits inside the 'shell'. Use general-purpose pliers to close the calotte and attach it to the clasp.

TIP

To make sure slack is taken up on wire or thread after threading is completed, hold the necklace up, as shown, before attaching the final part of the clasp.

Stiffening Beading Thread

When using beading thread, you will need either to use a needle for threading or stiffen the thread with superglue. For the latter, dip the first 5cm (2in) of one end of your thread into a bottle of liquid superglue. Allow a second or two for it to penetrate the thread, then remove it and swiftly wipe off the excess with a tissue. The thread will now be stiff enough for threading, but it will also be helpful to cut across it diagonally to provide a sharp point. (Be careful not to get any glue on your fingers!)

Using Thong or Cord with Box Calottes and Jump Rings

There are various styles of necklace end available for use with thong, but they all work by covering the end of the thong, secured in place by being squeezed onto the thong with pliers. The technique here uses a box calotte, which is both neat and effective, and suitable for all types of thong, such as leather, suede, cotton cord, rat-tail, ribbon or handmade cords. It can also be used for multiple lengths of suede or cord.

1 Using a pair of flat-nosed or general-purpose pliers, bend first one side of the box calotte, then the other side, over and down onto the thong or cord (diagram A).

2 Using a pair of general-purpose pliers, open a jump ring sideways (if possible, never pull a jump ring or other wire loop apart at the joint, as this weakens the link). Thread the jump ring through the loop of the box calotte, then thread on one part of the clasp (diagram B). Use the pliers to close the calotte.

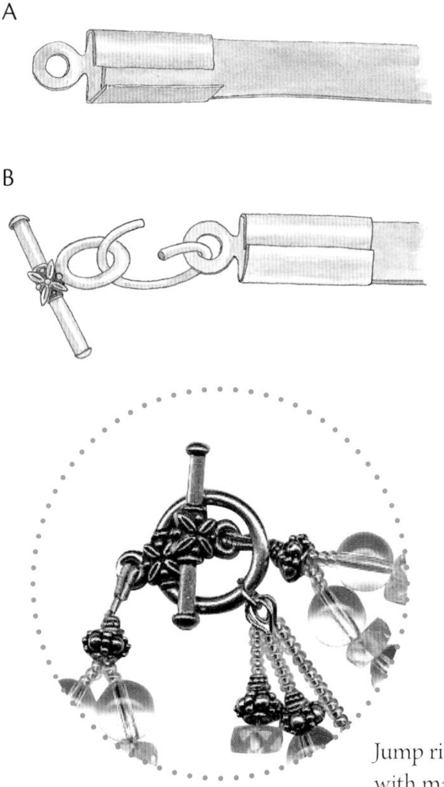

Jump rings are useful connectors with many applications.

Basic Earring Making

Most beaded earring designs are based on simply threading beads onto headpins and bending wires to form loops for linking beaded headpins together. However, some people do find forming perfect loops in wire a challenge, and for that reason I grade most earring projects with a 3 for ease of making. This and other earring-making techniques shown here are also used for making necklace drops, pendants or necklace clasp decorations.

Using Headpins

1 Select your beads and thread them onto a headpin (usually 5cm/2in, but other sizes are available) (diagram A).

2 Use flat-nosed pliers to bend the wire over at a right angle close to the top bead (diagram B).

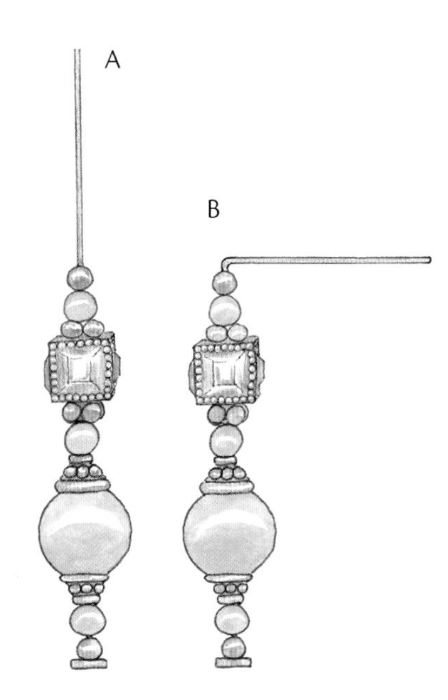

3 Use cutting pliers to trim off any spare wire, leaving about 8–10mm (less than ½in) (diagram C).

4 Use round-nosed pliers to form a loop – do this gradually, rather than in one motion (diagrams D and E).

5 If you are using a ready-made pair of ear-hooks, -studs or -clips, open the loop just made sideways, as for a jump ring (see left), and attach to the ear-fitting.

6 Alternatively, use straight-leg (unfinished) ear-hooks, to which you can add your own coordinating beads, as shown in diagrams F and G, and following Steps 2 and 4 left and above to form a loop.

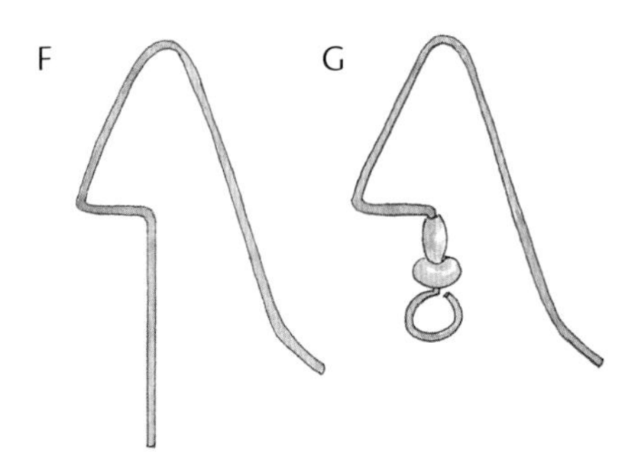

Using Multiple Headpins

Many of the earrings in this book are made using several headpins, which are looped together or onto spacers (diagrams A–C).

Another example of multiple headpin use.

Using Nylon-coated Wire with Crimp Beads

The same technique used for Basic Necklace Stringing, page 14, can applied to earring-making, as in diagrams A and B.

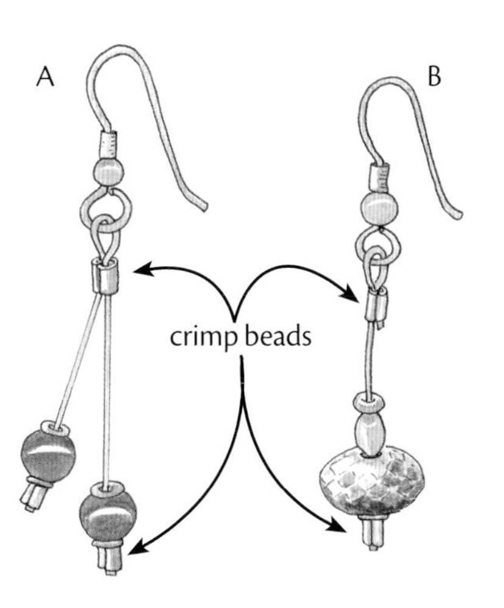

Using Nylon-coated Wire with Gimp and Crimp Beads

The same technique as in Basic Necklace Stringing, page 15, can be used in earring-making, with the beads threaded like a mini necklace onto wire, then both wire ends passing through the top beads and gimp to form a loop and make an attachment (diagram A). Note: The wire used must be fine (28 gauge).

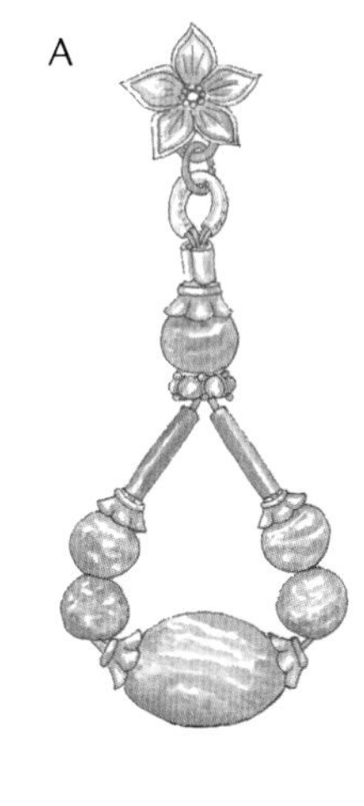

Recipe Notes

- If just 'bead' is listed in the ingredients lists, you should assume this to be round; all other shapes/types of bead are specifically described, e.g. cube, oval or rondel.

- Where metal items are specified as 'gold' or 'silver,' i.e. within quotation marks, this indicates that they are imitation gold or silver.

- When rocaille or bugle beads are listed in the ingredients, quantities may not be specified, as they are always purchased by weight or by the packet.

- Whenever reference is made to 'thread' or 'threading' in a method, this refers to the type of threading medium specified in the ingredients, such as nylon-coated wire, waxed cotton cord, thong and so on.

- Assume that the width of the 'thread' required is medium, unless otherwise stated in the ingredients lists.

- Equivalent imperial measurements for metric are normally given to the nearest ¼in, although for some larger measurements, the imperial figure is rounded up or down.

TIP

When working with niobium, cover the jaws of your pliers with clear adhesive tape to protect the anodized colour finish.

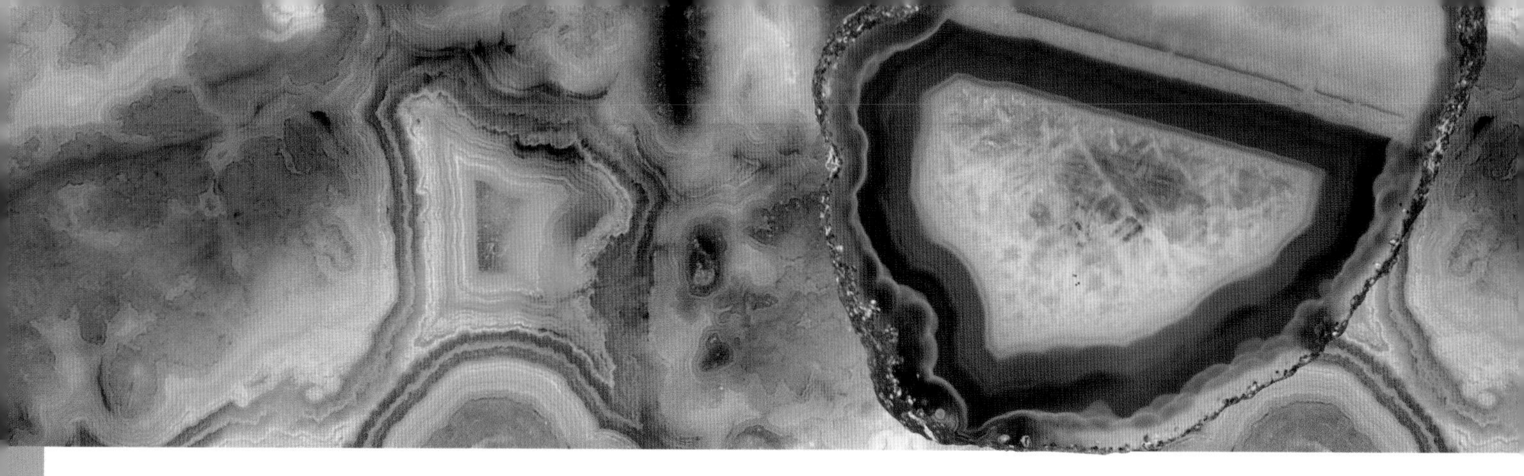

Agate

Agate is one of the most commonly available materials for the bead maker, and within the broad term 'agate' there are many contrasting varieties to be found. Indeed, some are so striking that I have featured them in their own right. However, the other agates are just as beautiful in their own way and this general agate chapter introduces just a few.

Because agate is so readily available, it is easy to understand why it was one of the first ornamental stones used by man for personal adornment, and perhaps it is for this reason that it has become a stone with a multitude of meanings and attributes. In this respect, it is considered to be a stone of courage, longevity, truth, protection, healing and self-confidence.

One of the birthstones for Gemini, agate confers various benefits on those born under this sign, as this delightful little rhyme relates: *'Gemini's children health and wealth command, And all the ills of age withstand, Who wear their rings on either hand of Agate.'*

Agate is often dyed and it is possible to find it in all sorts of artificial colours. The string of ancient agate beads shown below illustrates some of the wide variety of natural agate colours available, and one oval bead near the bottom of the page displays one of the most desirable features that this stone sometimes exhibits. Look closely and you will find just one with banding that looks rather like an eye; beads such as this are believed to be especially lucky.

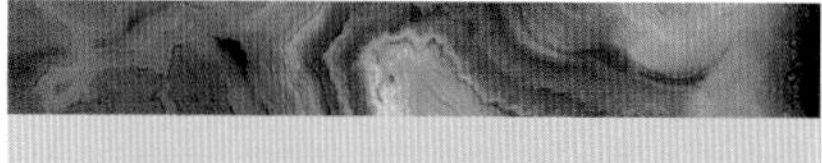

APPEARANCE AND COLOUR
Clear or translucent; brown, pink, blue and white

AVAILABILITY IN BEAD FORM
Common

COUNTRIES OF ORIGIN
Most parts of the world, especially Africa, Brazil, Czech Republic, India, Morocco, USA

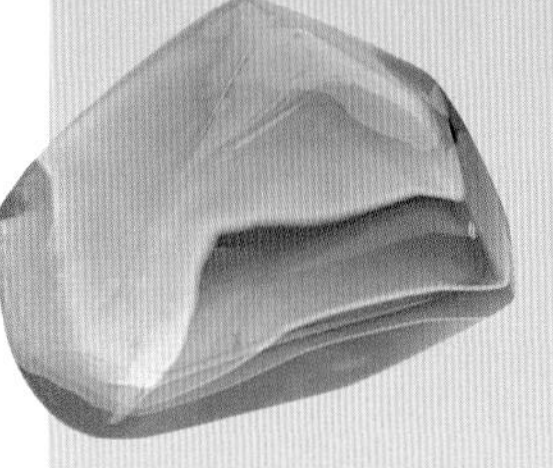

BUYER'S GUIDE

Agate is usually inexpensive, and even large and elaborate beads are available at a cost that compares favourably with quality glass beads.

Dream On

Time to make 1 hour • **Ease of making** 4 • **Length** 69cm (27in)

Hold these beads up to the light and it is easy to see why they are called dream agate! The translucent shades of light and dark, which range from milky grey and deep amber through to black, are arranged in flowing bands of colour that have a dream-like quality.

The necklace is easy and quick to make, in addition to being beautiful to wear, as it sits so flatteringly smooth against the skin.

INGREDIENTS

- 40cm (16in) string of flat oval dream agate beads, 35 x 22mm
- 10 gold-plated fancy disc beads, 5mm
- 1 gold-plated 'S' clasp
- 2 gold-plated box calottes
- 2 gold-plated jump rings
- 1m (39in) length of brown 1mm waxed cotton cord
- 2 x 60cm (24in) lengths of brown 1mm waxed cotton cord

A

1 Lay out the large beads in order of threading on a tray. Make sure that you choose any larger beads for the centre of the necklace.

2 Thread the beads onto the long length of waxed cotton cord and slide them to the centre of the cord, with two equal lengths at either end.

3 Tie a loose overhand knot close to the last bead on each side, then pass one of the shorter lengths of cord through each of the knots so that the centre of this length of cord is positioned in the knot (diagram A).

4 Tighten the knots, then plait (braid) the three lengths of cord together for a length of 15cm (6in), or until you have reached the length you require.

5 Trim all the cord ends to the same length, then apply a box calotte to cover the trimmed ends (see Using Thong or Cord with Box Calottes and Jump Rings, page 16).

6 Use a jump ring to attach one part of the clasp to one box calotte and attach the other jump ring to the remaining box calotte, then close it to provide a loop for fastening the necklace (see Using Thong or Cord with Box Calottes and Jump Rings, page 16). Be sure to open and close the jump rings sideways without pulling them apart, to avoid weakening the metal.

Agate geodes (hollow stones) are sometimes lined with sparkling crystals.

Sliced not Diced

One of the least expensive natural stone necklaces is the pendant, and sliced agate especially lends itself to this style. Agate is a stone that is easily dyed, and this process can confer dramatic colour, such as seen in the blue slice below. Agate slices are very easy to find and inexpensive. These two necklaces are made by the same simple method as the foregoing project, but without the plaiting (braiding) – follow those instructions to attach the box calottes.

Each necklace has a different type of cord. The turquoise is silky rat-tail, which can be purchased in a huge colour range from bead suppliers. The cream cord was a lucky find from a haberdashery store, which can yield some unusual threading materials.

Blue Elephant

Time to make 20 minutes • **Ease of making** 2 • **Length** 66cm (26in), plus 8cm (3in) drop

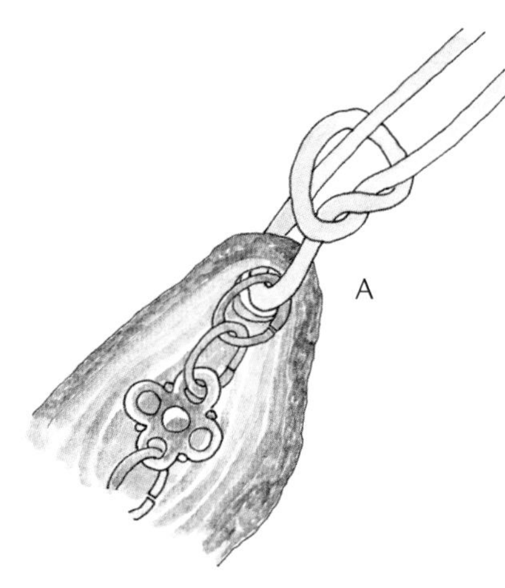

1 Attach the elephant drop to a 4-hole link with a jump ring, then attach two more jump rings to the top of the link.

2 Thread the length of rat-tail through the top jump ring and the agate slice, and then, after making sure that the pendant is in the centre of the length of rat-tail, tie an overhand knot with one side of the rat-tail around the other side (diagram A).

Coffee Slice

Time to make 15 minutes • **Ease of making** 3 • **Length** 41cm (16in), plus 6cm (2½in) drop

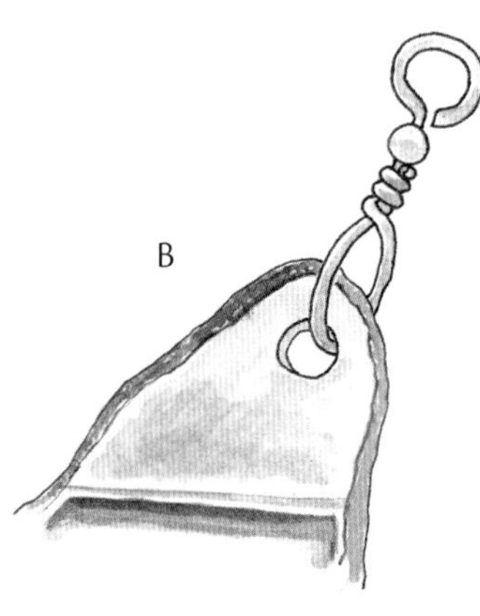

For this necklace, the agate slice is fixed to a bail with wire. Follow diagram B to make a double-looped wire attachment with a single 2mm sterling silver bead. Before applying the box calottes, simply thread the cord through the bail to suspend the pendant.

Botswana Double Act

Time to make 3 hours • **Ease of making** 6 • **Length** 76cm (30in), plus 10cm (4in) drops

As its name suggests, this Botswana agate originates from just one place: Botswana. It has an unmistakable overall smoky grey appearance, but within that general appearance it also has striking bands and waves of subtle colour, such as pinky browns and milky whites.

When I started making this project I intended it to be a chunky necklace, but while threading it occurred to me that it would also make a superb modern belt, so the clasp chosen is suitable for that purpose and the threading materials are strong yet supple enough to drape beautifully when used as a necklace.

The holes of the main beads were too small for threading onto waxed cotton cord, which would have been my threading medium of choice. Consequently, I chose strong beading thread for the threading of the large beads and then used this to tie in the other cord and faux suede.

INGREDIENTS

- ✧ 9 random-faceted Botswana agate beads, about 25 x 20mm
- ✧ 20 silver-plated large-holed beads (2 types)
- ✧ 6 silver-plated beads in mixed designs, 6–10mm
- ✧ 1 silver-plated 'S' clasp
- ✧ 2 silver-plated large box calottes
- ✧ 6 silver-plated small box calottes
- ✧ 2 silver-plated jump rings
- ✧ 6 silver-plated headpins
- ✧ 2 x 2m (79in) lengths of brown thick beading thread
- ✧ 2 x 1m (39in) lengths of faux suede, 1 grey, 1 tan
- ✧ 1m (39in) length of brown 1mm waxed cotton cord

A

1 Take one length of beading thread and one length of faux suede and tie one set of ends together with an overhand knot. You will need to undo this later, so do not pull it too tight.

2 Thread one of the silver-plated large-holed beads onto both the beading thread and the faux suede. About 15cm (6in) from the knotted end, use the beading thread to loop back through the bead and then tie it in an overhand knot around the faux suede (diagram A).

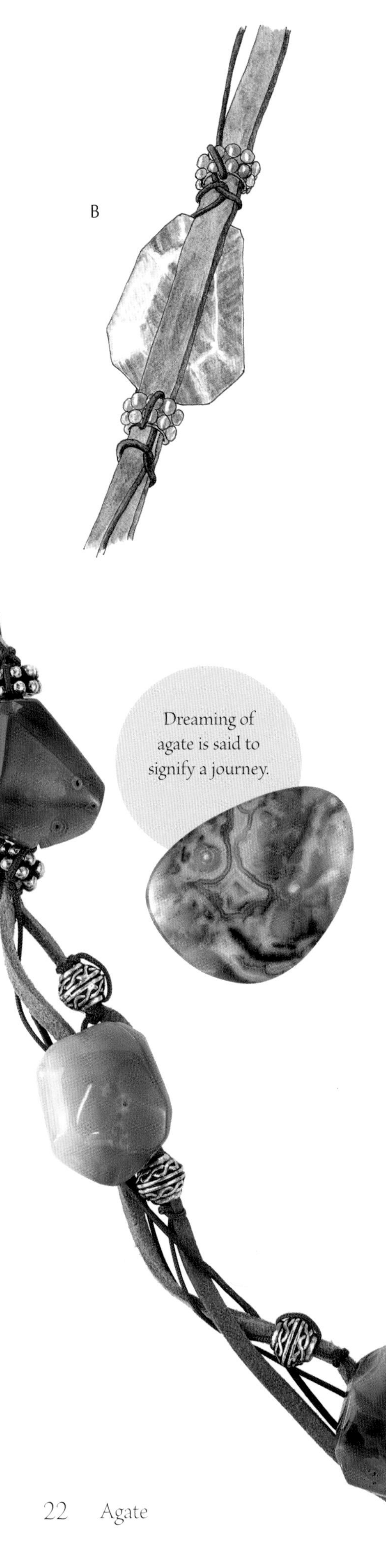

Dreaming of agate is said to signify a journey.

3 Thread one of the large agate beads onto the beading thread, then pass both threads together through another silver-plated large-holed bead.

4 As in Step 2, thread the beading thread back through the last threaded silver-plated bead and secure in place by tying an overhand knot around the faux suede. Your beads should now appear as in diagram B.

5 Repeat Steps 2–4 four more times, keeping the sequences of beads at roughly similar intervals and alternating the two different types of silver-plated bead threaded. Finish by loosely tying the ends of the beading thread and faux suede together.

6 Repeat Steps 1–5 with the other length of beading thread and faux suede using the remaining four agate beads, but make sure that they are in different positions on the thread/faux suede to the first beaded string.

7 Untie the knots made in Step 1 and pass one set of ends of both beaded strings of beading threads and faux suede through one of the remaining silver-plated large-holed beads. As in Step 2, secure in place about 8cm (3in) from the first bead threaded.

8 Apply a large box calotte close to the bead threaded in Step 7 over the ends of both beaded strings of beading threads and faux suede, and also include the length of waxed cotton cord (see Using Thong or Cord with Box Calottes and Jump Rings, page 16). A spare amount of the beading threads, faux suede and waxed cotton cord should be protruding from the box calotte to form the 'tassel'.

9 Make sure that the two lengths of beaded strings are of equal length, then repeat Step 7 with the other set of ends of the beaded strings of beading threads and faux suede.

10 Go back to the calotte end of the necklace, take the unthreaded waxed cotton cord and tie an overhand knot around all the threads and faux suede both in front of and after the first silver-plated bead. Then, in a spiral motion, loosely wind the cord around all the threaded lengths until you reach the other end of the necklace/belt. As before, tie a knot in front of and after the last silver-plated bead.

11 Repeat Step 8 to apply the other large box calotte over all the threading materials, then apply a jump ring to each calotte (see Using Thong or Cord with Box Calottes and Jump Rings, page 16). Loop the 'S' clasp through one of these jump rings and then use your pliers to close the clasp slightly to secure it in place.

12 Cut the spare threading materials to your required length (I left them uneven) and apply a small box calotte to each end of the faux suede and to the beading threads and waxed cotton cord together.

13 Thread a headpin through each of the remaining silver-plated beads, form a loop and attach a drop to each of the small calottes (see Using Headpins, page 16).

Some of the special attributes of this gentle-looking stone are a reputation for relieving depression, solving problems and helping smokers quit the dreaded weed!

Onyx Charmer

Time to make 40 minutes • **Ease of making** 3 • **Length** 15cm (6in)

Onyx is a form of agate that is often dyed, as in the case of the beads featured here. These are a beautiful shade of soft green, but often the dyed colour is much stronger and darker. This fun item is a handbag charm that is almost like a charm bracelet, and you could attach any of your favourite little pendants to it. Those that I have chosen are cute little gold-plated animals, which are sure to be loved by all who see them. The project is quite simple to make by using the photograph as a guide to threading and following the instructions for Using Thong or Cord with Box Calottes and Jump Rings, page 16. Note that where a length of cord has two beads, the top bead is kept in place with an overhand knot tied in the cord beneath it.

Moss agate is said to be the gardener's friend. If worn while tending plants, expect a bumper crop or beautiful blooms!

INGREDIENTS

- 9 onyx beads, 6–8mm
- 5 gold-plated animal pendants
- 1 gold-plated key-ring
- 6 gold-plated box calottes
- 5 gold-plated jump rings
- 5 x 6–11mm lengths of natural-coloured 1mm waxed cotton cord

Pick 'n' Mix

Time to make 1½ hours • **Ease of making** 3 • **Length** 15cm (6in), stretchy

This inexpensive, fun item of jewellery is a pleasure to wear and it incorporates many different agates together with hematine. At first glance, you may not realize that the beads are actually threaded onto humble safety pins! These are the standard design but nickel free, to avoid giving rise to allergies.

INGREDIENTS

- 110 mixed semi-precious stone beads, 4mm
- 84 hematine bicone beads, 5mm
- 42 nickel-free safety pins
- 2 gold-plated box calottes
- 2 x 30cm (12in) lengths of 'gold' elastic cord

1 Thread 21 safety pins with 4 hematine beads and 21 safety pins with the mixed 4mm round beads. Close each safety pin after threading, then use a pair of general-purpose pliers to squeeze the catch 'wings' of all the safety pins closed.

2 Thread a length of elastic cord through each hole at either end of the pins, threading on the hematine and mixed-bead pins alternately. Pull the cords so that they are not stretched and the pins are evenly distributed. Use the pliers to bend the loops of both box calottes inwards, then use to join each pair of ends of the two lengths of cord together (diagram A).

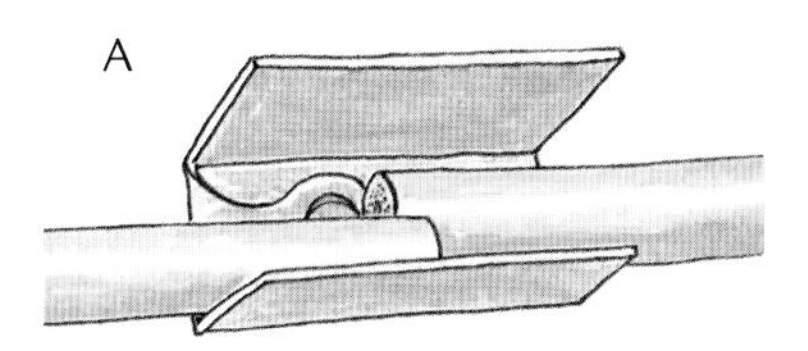

When making an item of jewellery from mixed stones such as these, why not combine according to their meanings? In this way, the Pick 'n' Mix bracelet could stand for, love, protection and peace.

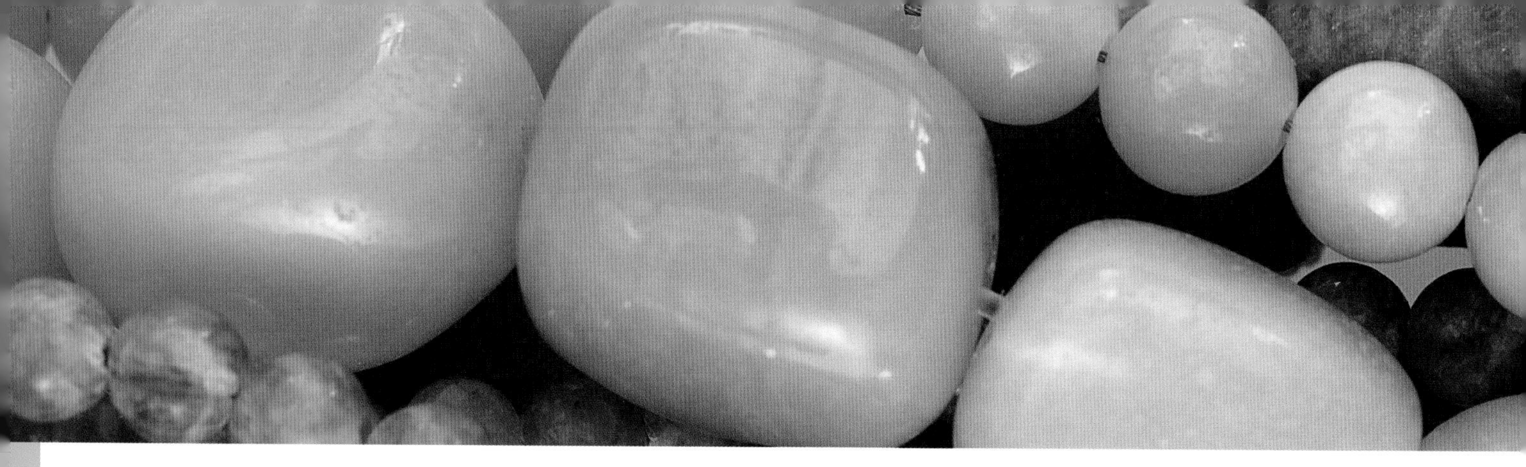

Amazonite

As I sit in front of my computer and type this chapter, the amazonite beads lie on my desk between me and the screen, and I think 'how appropriate', because one of the chief attributes of amazonite is considered to be an ability to provide protection from electromagnetic fields. Indeed, some people believe that we would all be well advised to tape a piece of this stone to our mobile (cell) phones.

Perhaps because of the natural landscape and its abundance of lush vegetation, we all seem to find the colour green restful, and this may be the reason why another power attributed to amazonite is the capacity to soothe and calm both the mind and body.

For those with problems to solve, amazonite may well prove beneficial, as it is reputed to bring clarity of view to a troubled situation and help those involved to see the issue from both sides.

In terms of its health-promoting properties, amazonite is believed to aid the skeletal and muscular system, and bring relief to those affected by tooth decay or osteoporosis.

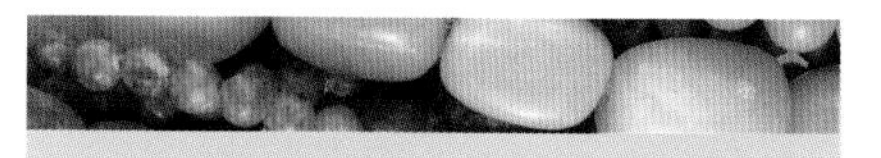

APPEARANCE AND COLOUR
Opaque shades of bluish green

AVAILABILITY IN BEAD FORM
Common

COUNTRIES OF ORIGIN
Austria, Brazil, Canada, China, India, Mozambique, Namibia, Russia

Power bracelets such as this are available in almost every stone type. They are normally inexpensive to buy and can be a good way to purchase beads for jewellery making.

BUYER'S GUIDE

Amazonite is usually available in two different greens. The paler version is invariably Chinese stone, while the stronger-coloured stone is normally from Russia.

Tzarina

Time to make 2 hours • **Ease of making** 4 • **Length** 56cm (22in)

From somewhere in the vast tracts of Russia, the raw material for these gorgeous spearmint green amazonite beads is mined and then sent to China for fashioning into beads.

I love the rough, chunky nature of these unpolished beads, and for contrast have teamed them with both baroque and perfect round beads. These three in combination look great when teamed with a few 'silver' accent beads.

The necklace is simple and surprisingly inexpensive to make, and as an alternative could feature only two of the strands, choosing any combination you prefer.

INGREDIENTS

- 40cm (16in) string of rough amazonite beads, 12–15mm
- 40cm (16in) string of baroque amazonite beads, 9–10mm
- 40cm (16in) string of amazonite beads, 4mm
- 2 Chinese 'silver' lantern beads, 20 x 10mm
- 1 Chinese 'silver' round bead, 15mm
- 6 silver-plated cushion beads, 10mm
- 9 silver-plated fancy square beads, 6mm
- 6 silver-plated fancy cushion beads, 4mm
- 2 silver-plated 3–1 necklace ends
- 1 silver-plated toggle clasp
- 6 inexpensive 'silver' crimp beads for use as temporary 'stoppers'
- 6 'silver' crimp beads
- 2 silver-plated jump rings
- 6 x 8mm (⅜in) lengths of 'silver' gimp
- 66cm (26in) length of thick nylon-coated wire
- 2 x 56cm (22in) lengths of nylon-coated wire

1 Thread one of the inexpensive crimp beads onto the length of thick nylon-coated wire and secure it to one end of the wire with your pliers (see Using Nylon-coated Wire with Crimp Beads, page 14).

2 Thread the sequence of beads shown in the photograph for the outer strand onto the wire, but if using different beads than the ones specified, thread for a length of 50cm (19¾in). Secure a crimp bead to the other end of the wire, as in Step 1.

As an alternative to the more traditional power bracelet, the larger-bead versions, such as the one opposite, are now easy to find and provide about 50 x 12–15mm cushion-shaped

3 Repeat Steps 1 and 2 to thread the central strand of beads, but if using different beads than the ones specified, thread for a length of 43cm (17in).

4 Repeat Steps 1 and 2 with the smallest, inner strand of beads, but if using different beads than the ones specified, thread for a length of 39cm (15½in).

5 Hold all three strands together against your neck and check that the beads hang to the correct length for you. After making any necessary adjustments, i.e. adding or removing beads, use the 'silver' crimp beads and the gimp to attach the beaded strands to the relevant holes of the 3–1 necklace ends (see Using Nylon-coated Wire with Gimp and Crimp Beads, page 15).

6 Use the two jump rings to attach the clasp to the single holes of the 3–1 necklace ends (see Using Thong or Cord with Box Calottes and Jump Rings, page 16), taking care to open and close the jump rings sideways.

Summer Wedding

Time to make 6 hours • **Ease of making** 7 • **Length** 40cm (16in), plus 10cm (4in) bead net drop

This project appears to be a bit of a challenge to bring you so early in the book, so novices may just take fright and turn the page, but don't worry, just follow the simple instructions and you can make this beautiful necklace – it is not as difficult as it looks! The beads used are inexpensive Chinese amazonite with a lovely soft green hue, and I can just imagine the necklace as the perfect complement to a creamy wedding outfit. The fluttering ribbons hanging from the clasp are optional, so those who would prefer a plainer look can simply cut off the spare ribbon after attaching the clasp.

INGREDIENTS

- 1 Chinese amazonite bead, 6mm
- 2 x 40cm (16in) strands of Chinese amazonite beads, 4mm
- 58 silver-plated fancy cushion beads, 4mm
- 7 silver-plated bead caps, 3mm
- 1 silver-plated toggle clasp
- 7 'silver' crimp beads
- 7 inexpensive crimp beads for use as temporary 'stoppers'
- 2 silver-plated box calottes
- 2 silver-plated jump rings
- 45cm (17¾in) length of fine nylon-coated wire
- 2 x 30cm (12in) lengths of fine nylon-coated wire
- 2 x 25cm (10in) lengths of nylon-coated wire
- 2 x 20cm (8in) lengths of nylon-coated wire
- 2 x 72cm (28in) lengths of cream 4mm ribbon
- 2 x 72cm (28in) lengths of pale green 4mm ribbon

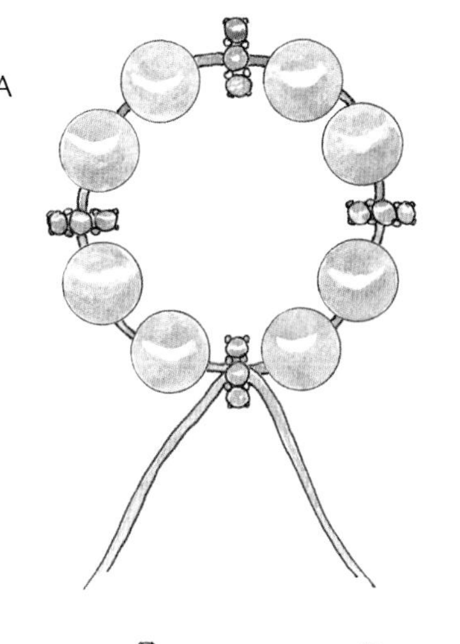

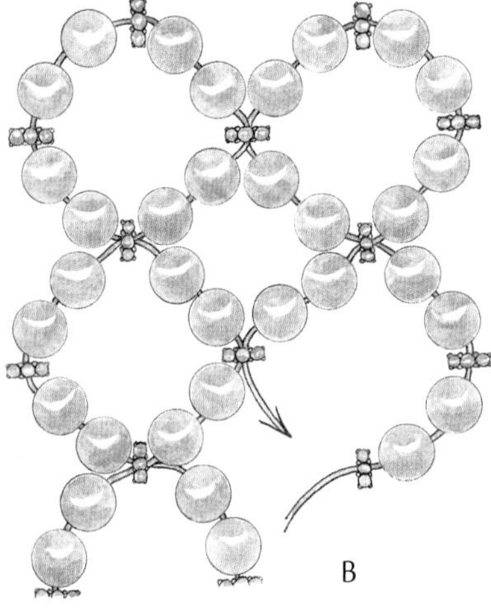

1 Thread two 4mm amazonite beads and one cushion bead onto the 45cm (17¾in) length of nylon-coated wire, then repeat three times. Slide these beads to the centre of the length of wire, then thread both ends of the wire through the last threaded cushion bead from opposite directions (diagram A).

2 Thread two amazonite, one cushion and two more amazonite beads onto each wire end, then thread both ends through another cushion bead from opposite directions. Repeat three more times.

3 Thread on the 6mm amazonite bead followed by a 3mm bead cap and a 'silver' crimp bead. Do not secure the crimp bead in place, but thread on an inexpensive crimp bead and, leaving the threaded beads with some movement on the wire, secure in place by squeezing with general-purpose pliers.

4 Thread two amazonite beads onto one of the 30cm (12in) lengths of nylon-coated wire, then thread up through one of the side cushion beads at the top of the first threading. Continue threading in the same sequence as Step 1, finishing by threading in opposite directions through the last cushion bead (diagram B).

5 Continue threading with a cushion bead between every set of two amazonite beads and linking threads by passing one end of the wire down through the side cushion bead of the first threading (diagram B). Complete the threading after the fourth threading sequence by repeating Step 3, but replace the 6mm amazonite bead with a 4mm amazonite bead.

6 Repeat Steps 4 and 5 on the other side of the first threading.

7 Repeat Steps 4–6 on either side of the second and third threadings with the 25cm (10in) lengths of nylon-coated wire and using only three beading sequences. Repeat once more either side of the previous two threadings with the remaining lengths of wire and using only two beading sequences.

8 Lay your threaded beads on a flat surface in front of you and pull the wires gently so that the beads take up most of the slack and sit evenly on both sides. Use pliers (preferably crimp pliers) to secure the 'silver' crimp beads in place. Use a pair of sharp cutting pliers to cut off all the spare wire together with the temporary crimp beads.

9 Attach a cream and a green ribbon to each side of the necklace by threading through the outer 'rings' of beads and tying an overhand knot. Choose the length that you require for your necklace by holding it up to your neck. In your chosen position, apply a box calotte over the four lengths of ribbon on each side, then attach the clasp to the necklace with jump rings, remembering to open and close them sideways (see Using Thong or Cord with Box Calottes and Jump Rings, page 16).

10 If you are keeping the ribbons long, trim them at an angle to varying lengths with a sharp pair of scissors, or if you prefer the necklace without ribbons, use your pliers to trim them close to the clasp.

Flower Power

Time to make 30 minutes• **Ease of making** 3 • **Length** 5cm (2in)

INGREDIENTS

- 2 baroque amazonite beads, 9–10mm
- 10 amazonite beads, 4mm
- 4 frosted teal-coloured bugle beads, 10mm
- 10 silver-plated bead caps, 3mm
- 2 silver-plated fancy cushion beads, 4mm
- 2 'silver' crimp beads
- 2 silver-plated jump rings
- 1 pair of silver-plated ear-studs
- 1 pair of silver-plated clutch-backs for ear-studs
- 2 x 8mm (⅜in) lengths of 'silver' gimp
- 2 x 15cm (6in) lengths of fine nylon-coated wire

This gorgeous pair of drop earrings were designed to match Tzarina, but stand equally well alone. They are made using the leftover amazonite beads from the necklace, strung on fine nylon-coated wire like a mini necklace, with the two ends of wire brought together to form a loop. Both ends are threaded through the beads at the top of the drop and then, using gimp and crimp beads, treated as one to form a loop and attached to the jump ring (see Using Nylon-coated Wire with Gimp and Crimp Beads, pages 15 and 17).

Amber

A few pieces of the most prized amber hold perfectly preserved insects that could be up to 100 million years old!

Amber sneaks into this book under false pretences because in reality it is not a stone at all but the fossilized remains of ancient tree resin. However, it has been highly regarded and treasured by man for many thousands of years, and finds from Stone Age burial places reveal that it was one of the earliest stones used for adornment. Today, it is still treasured and known as a gemstone.

Unlike all other stones, amber is warm to the touch, and this led to our forefathers linking it with life and the energy of nature.

It also has the ability to become electrically charged when subjected to the friction of soft materials and consequently will attract small particles to itself.

As a good luck, protective, magical and healing 'stone' it has few parallels, and it is also said that those who wear amber have enhanced beauty and attract more friends and love into their lives.

It can be difficult to distinguish real amber from fake, but a few simple tests might help. Apply a hot needle to the inside of a bead, and if the resulting scent is resinous, your bead is most likely to be amber, as plastic beads give off an acrid smell. Rub your bead against some soft material, preferably wool or silk, and if it then attracts particles of dust, it is probably the real thing. But the best policy of all is to purchase new beads from a reliable source.

According to Chinese legend, amber was created by the solidified souls of deceased tigers!

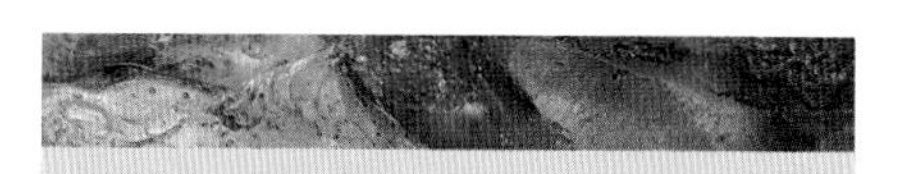

APPEARANCE AND COLOUR
Opaque to clear in shades of golden yellow to chestnut brown

AVAILABILITY IN BEAD FORM
Easily available

COUNTRIES OF ORIGIN
Dominica, Germany, Italy, Poland, Romania, Russia, UK

BUYER'S GUIDE

Most amber is in the medium price range, although some examples, such as the necklaces shown on the left, and items containing preserved insects (see above) are relatively expensive.

Lazy Bracelet

Time to make 1 hour • **Ease of making** 5 • **Length** 21cm (8¼in)

I call this project Lazy Bracelet because all the tumble-chip beads remain exactly as I purchased them and are on their original string. I have simply folded the string of beads in two so that four strands run parallel to each other and have then bound them all together with a threaded strand of rocailles and silver-plated beads.

The most inexpensive way to purchase amber is in tumble-chip form, but it always looks its best when seen as a large piece, so here you have the best of both worlds. The bracelet is inexpensive to make and its chunky form gives the appearance of much larger beads.

INGREDIENTS

- 85cm (33½in) string of tumble-chip amber beads, without clasp
- amber-coloured AB-coated rocaille beads
- 9 silver-plated fancy cube beads
- 1 silver-plated toggle clasp
- 4 'silver' crimp beads
- 1 inexpensive crimp bead for use as a temporary 'stopper'
- 2 silver-plated jump rings
- 2 x 2cm (5in) lengths of 'silver' gimp
- 55cm (21½in) length of fine nylon-coated wire

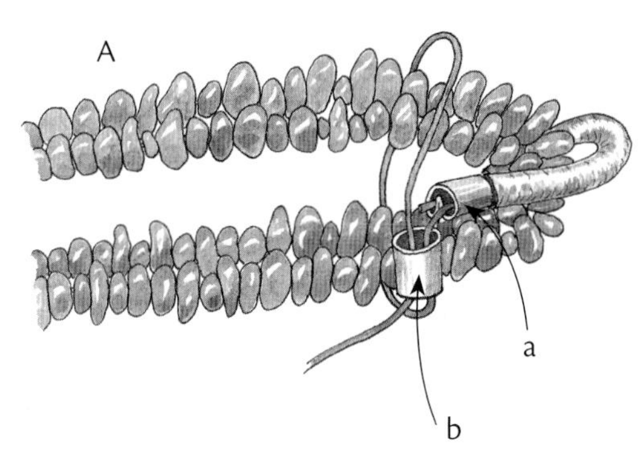

1 Fold the string of beads in two so that you have four continuous strands together. Thread one of the lengths of gimp onto the nylon-coated wire. Thread the wire and gimp through the loops of beads at one end, then thread both ends of the wire through a 'silver' crimp bead ('a' in diagram A). Keep one end close to the crimp bead.

2 Pull the wire tight so that the loops of beads are caught up in a firm (but not too tight) loop of gimp-covered wire. Fix this in place by squeezing the crimp bead with a pair of general-purpose pliers. Trim the spare wire from the short end of the wire.

3 Thread on another 'silver' crimp bead ('b' in diagram A). Pass the wire around the four strands of beads and back through the crimp bead. Pull the wire tight before fixing the crimp bead in place with your pliers.

4 Thread 10 rocaille beads followed by a silver-plated cube bead onto the long end of the wire. Repeat eight times, then thread on an inexpensive crimp bead and fix in place with your pliers.

5 Twist the strands of amber together and then wind (in the opposite direction to the twist of the amber beads) the threaded strand of rocaille beads around the twisted strands of amber. When you reach the far end, you may discover that you need to add or remove some of the rocaille beads to make this strand the same length to match the amber. This is because tumble-chip beads are of varying sizes and yours could be smaller or larger than the ones used here. Remove the temporary crimp bead and add or remove beads as necessary.

6 Repeat Step 3 at this end of the bracelet. Then thread on one more 'silver' crimp bead and the remaining length of gimp, thread the gimp and wire through the looped beads and thread back through the crimp bead to form a loop. Use your pliers to secure the crimp bead and then trim any spare wire.

7 Complete the bracelet by attaching the clasp with a jump ring looped through both the clasp and loop of gimp at either end (see Using Thong or Cord with Box Calottes and Jump Rings, page 16).

Simplicity

Time to make 1 hour • **Ease of making** 4 • **Length** 43cm (17in)

There is nothing like a plain string of knotted amber beads for a tactile appeal. The beads feel soft and warm to the touch, and the drape of the necklace cannot be bettered.

For those new to knotting, this is an easy introduction, as I have used a fairly thick thread that only needs a single overhand knot, and the beads are relatively large, so you won't need to make many knots!

It is said that amber is most beneficial when worn at the neck or wrist, so this necklace, which is of choker length, is perfect for those who wish to take advantage of its magical powers.

INGREDIENTS

- 40cm (16in) string of amber beads (graduated in size 15 x 10mm–10 x 8mm)
- 1 silver-plated toggle clasp
- 2 'silver' clamshell calottes
- 90cm (35in) length of thick beading thread in a matching colour to the beads
- bottle of liquid superglue

As amber is one of the main birthstones for those born under the sign of Leo, this necklace would make a perfect gift for a special birthday for anyone with an appropriate birth date.

TIP

When knotting a necklace, I always allow well over double the length of beading thread to the amount of beads used, as there is nothing more frustrating than coming to the end of the thread before your necklace is completed and wasting all that time!

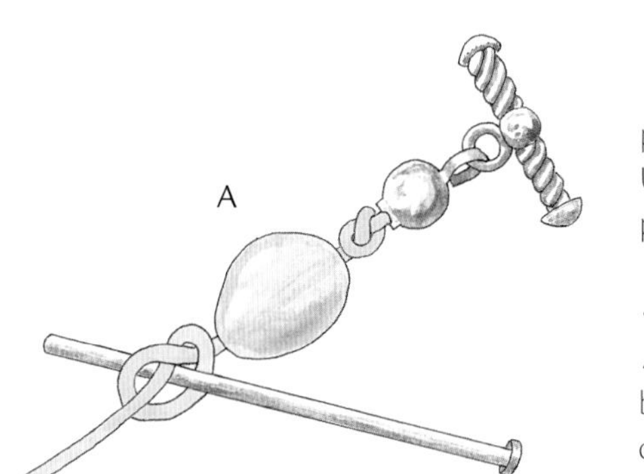

1 Stiffen the beading thread with superglue (see page 15), then attach one end to one part of the clasp with a clamshell calotte (see Using Beading Thread with Clamshell Calottes, page 15).

2 Tie an overhand knot close to the calotte and then thread on a bead. Push this bead up to the last knot and then tie another overhand knot close to the bead (diagram A). It is sometimes helpful to use a strong headpin, or something similar, to help place the knot close to the bead.

3 Continue in this way until all the beads are threaded and then apply the remaining clamshell calotte, as in Step 1. Finish off by attaching the calotte to the other part of the clasp (diagram A).

Droplets

Time to make 1 hour • **Ease of making** 3 • **Length** 46cm (18in), plus 2.5cm (1in) drops

Droplets offers another inexpensive way of incorporating the magic of amber into an item of jewellery, and here I have used just one amber bead, left over from Simplicity (see opposite), and combined it with amber-coloured Swarovski crystal beads and silver-plated charms to make an interesting modern necklace.

The necklace is simple to make for those who have mastered the art of forming loops in wire, but is a little time-consuming because so many loops need to be made.

INGREDIENTS

- 1 amber bead, 10 x 9mm
- 3 Swarovski Colorado Topaz crystal beads, 6mm
- 4 Swarovski Colorado Topaz crystal beads, 5mm
- 3 Swarovski Colorado Topaz crystal beads, 4mm
- 8 silver-plated charms
- 4 amber-coloured AB-coated rocaille beads
- 4 'gold' bugle beads
- 34 sterling silver beads, 2mm
- 14 silver-plated beaded washer beads, 3mm
- 9 sterling silver jump rings
- 27 sterling silver headpins, 25mm (if available, to save on cost)
- 46cm (18in) length of heavyweight sterling silver chain

1 Make up little droplets of beads on the headpins, using the photograph as a guide to threading and following the instructions for Using Headpins, page 16. Make up one longer droplet using the large amber bead as the central feature.

2 Open a jump ring sideways and attach three droplets, including the central drop (see Using Thong or Cord with Box Calottes and Jump Rings, page 16). Before closing the jump ring, attach it to the central link of the chain.

3 Attach three droplets to each of the remaining jump rings and attach to links on the chain, ensuring as far as possible that these are all attached to the same side of the links on the chain so that the drops hang correctly. I have left one clear link between each droplet, but you may prefer to leave more for a less-dense look. To achieve the effect shown here, use the longer droplets for the centre of the necklace.

Beware, amber is often imitated, and many strings of old beads that purport to be amber are not the real thing at all. The two examples seen here are old and attractive, but not amber.

Amethyst

Amethyst is said to promote happiness, love, healing, peace, courage, intelligence, justice, peaceful sleep, pleasant dreams and even successful business dealings. It is also believed to enhance spiritual awareness and relieve stress. When worn or carried, it is supposed to focus the mind, bring clarity and aid studying. Especially beneficial for travellers, it protects the wearer from robbery, danger and illness.

These many attributes, together with its beauty, make amethyst a popular and suitable gift for almost anyone. But it is particularly appropriate for a romantic gift, as it is regarded as a stone for lovers. When given by sweetheart to sweetheart, it is reputed to strengthen their emotional bond. A silver-mounted amethyst heart given by a woman to a man is believed to ensure that their love endures. A word of caution, though – it is said that a man who wears amethyst is attractive to 'good women'!

In its natural state, amethyst is a spectacular stone, although its beauty is often hidden within a geode. These hollow stones give the outward appearance of normal yet lightweight stone, ranging in size from just a few centimetres or inches to several metres or feet in diameter, which only reveal their crystal treasures – often types other than amethyst – when opened. You may be lucky and find one intact, but I have searched for many years and only found broken specimens.

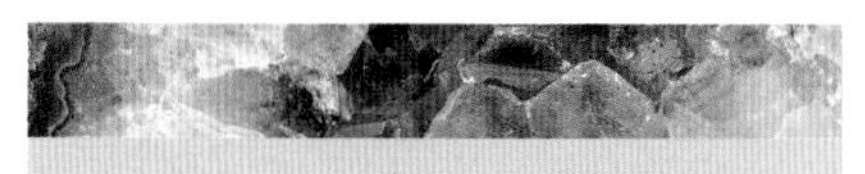

APPEARANCE AND COLOUR
Pointed crystals of clear to translucent pale violet to deep purple

AVAILABILITY IN BEAD FORM
Common; clear deep colours are relatively expensive

COUNTRIES OF ORIGIN
Brazil, Canada, East Africa, India, Mexico, Russia, Siberia, Sri Lanka, UK, USA

BUYER'S GUIDE

Amethyst is ideal for the newcomer to semi-precious stone, as it is widely available and found in a range of bead types and prices, from inexpensive to moderate.

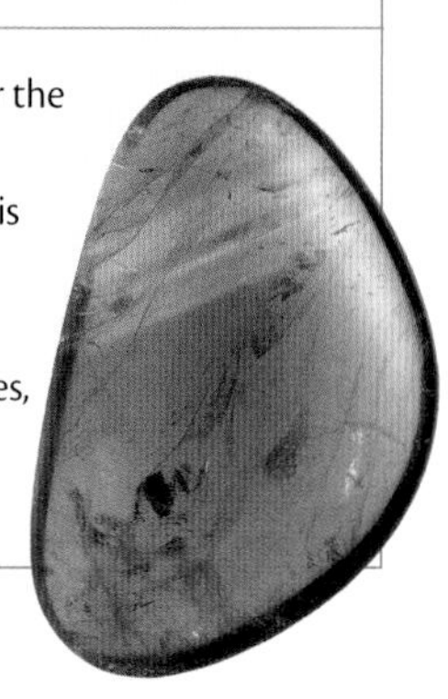

Wild Iris

Time to make 2 hours • **Ease of making** 3 • **Length** 69cm (27in)

With all the varied colours of its namesake, this necklace displays amethyst beautifully. The large, shaped beads exhibit a wonderful depth of colour, while contrasting small beads add clarity and delicacy.

The necklace is highly adaptable and has no clasp; instead, a simple loop slides up or down the string of beads, allowing easy adjustment of length and variation of style.

INGREDIENTS

- 40cm (16in) string of baroque faceted flat amethyst beads, about 30 x 15mm
- 14 cubed or faceted amethyst beads, 6mm
- 40cm (16in) string of amethyst beads, 2mm
- 12 gold-plated rondel beads, 6 x 4mm
- 2 gold-plated 4-hole links
- 1 gold-plated cone-shaped bead cap
- 4 'gold' crimp beads
- 3 gold-plated headpins
- 80cm (32in) length of nylon-coated wire
- 45cm (18in) length of nylon-coated wire

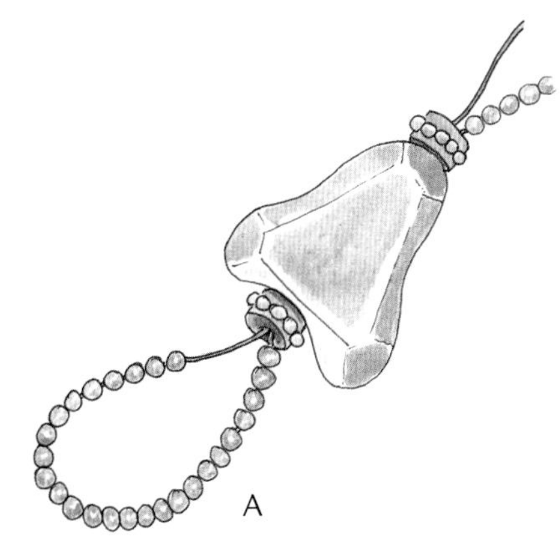

1 Attach the 45cm (18in) length of nylon-coated wire to a loop of one of the 4-hole links using a crimp bead (see Using Nylon-coated Wire with Crimp Beads, page 14). Using the photograph of the necklace as a guide, thread on beads and the cone-shaped bead cap as shown to make the single strand. When you have threaded the last bead, attach the remaining 4-hole link using a crimp bead as before.

2 To make the mini tassel, again using the photograph of the necklace as a guide, thread beads onto the three headpins, trim the lengths of the headpins, then attach to the remaining holes of the second 4-hole link (see Using Headpins, page 16, and Using Multiple Headpins, page 17).

3 Attach one end of the remaining length of nylon-coated wire to the first 4-hole link as in Step 1, but this time to one of the side holes. Thread on four 2mm amethyst beads, one gold-plated rondel bead, eleven 2mm amethyst beads, one gold-plated rondel bead and one large amethyst bead. Thread the same sequence of beads, excluding the first four 2mm amethyst beads, four more times.

4 After threading the last large amethyst, thread one more gold-plated rondel bead and 26 more 2mm amethyst beads. The latter number of beads may need to be adjusted to form a loop that suits the size of your large beads, i.e. the loop needs to be able to slide over the beads but not be too loose.

5 Pass the thread up through the last rondel bead, the large amethyst bead and the next rondel bead (diagram A).

6 Thread on eleven 2mm amethyst beads, then repeat Step 5. Continue in the same way three more times, then thread on eleven 2mm amethyst beads, pass the thread up through the rondel bead on the other strand, then thread on four 2mm amethyst beads. After adjusting the wire to take up most of the slack, attach this end to the remaining side hole of the 4-hole link using the remaining crimp bead as in Step 1.

Graceful

Time to make 1 hour • **Ease of making** 3 • **Length** 56cm (22in)

Graceful is a necklace and earrings set of delicate appearance. The earrings are made from amethyst teardrop beads, while the necklace combines amethyst with ametrine. The latter are the large beads in the necklace and you will notice that they combine a golden hue with pale purple. This type of stone comes from one mine only in the world, in Bolivia, but is readily available in bead form at a moderate cost.

Ametrine is a combination of amethyst and citrine, the latter contributing the golden tinge, and has characteristics that make it especially desirable for those seeking the magical powers of stones. It is said that ametrine embraces the attributes of both stones in a particularly powerful way (see page 52 for further information on citrine). Perhaps because two colours of quartz are combined in harmony within this stone, it is believed that it confers compatibility and a trust in others. Ametrine is also reputed to have many health-promoting benefits, such as relieving the effects of chronic fatigue, depression and stress-related diseases.

The beads are threaded onto nylon-coated wire with a difference. Although made from the customary steel, this 'gold' variety has a coating of 24-carat gold over the wire and beneath the clear nylon, making it both durable and attractive as well as suitable for this particular style of necklace, where the wire is meant to be seen.

Amethyst has a reputation for preventing inebriation. The 13th-century writer Ragiel reported: *'A bear, if engraved on an amethyst, has the virtue of putting demons to flight and preserves the wearer from drunkenness.'*

INGREDIENTS

- 40cm (16in) string (or 6 beads) of randomly faceted ametrine beads, about 20 x 12mm
- 40cm (16in) string of teardrop amethyst beads, about 12 x 6mm
- 7 baroque amethyst beads, 10mm
- 35 gold-plated thin rondel beads, 4mm
- 1 gold-plated toggle clasp
- 33 goldfill crimp beads
- 68cm (27in) length of 'gold' nylon-coated wire
- 63cm (25in) length of 'gold' nylon-coated wire
- 55cm (22in) length of 'gold' nylon-coated wire

1 Using the photograph of the necklace as a guide, thread the central sequence of beads onto the 55cm (22in) length of wire for the inner strand of the necklace and slide them to the centre of the wire. Using the crimp beads, fix the sequence of beads in place, preferably using a pair of specialist crimp pliers to give a neat finish (see Using Nylon-coated Wire with Crimp Beads, page 14).

2 Leaving a gap of 5cm (2in) from one end of the bead sequence, apply another crimp bead to the wire and then thread on beads as shown in the photograph. Secure in place by applying another crimp bead. Repeat for the other side of the strand.

3 Using the photograph of the necklace as a guide, thread the two central sequences of beads onto the 63mm (25in) length of wire for the middle strand of the necklace, leaving a gap of 1.5cm (⅝in) between the two beaded sections and applying a crimp bead at either end, as in Step 2.

4 Leave a gap of 3.2cm (1¼in) either side of the beads just threaded, then apply another crimp bead. Using the photograph of the necklace as a guide, thread on the second two sequences of beads. Apply crimp beads to secure in place, as before.

5 Using the photograph of the necklace as a guide, thread the remaining length of wire with the bead sequences shown for the outer strand of the necklace, leaving a gap of 2cm (¾in) either side of the central beads and 3cm (1⅛in) before the two outer bead sequences and securing each bead sequence in place with crimp beads, as before.

6 Thread a crimp bead onto the three wires together at either end of the necklace. Hold the necklace to your neck to choose the lengths you require for each strand and slide each crimp bead into the required position. Secure each crimp bead in place with pliers, as before.

7 Because this wire is fairly thick, and six thicknesses will not go through one crimp bead, it is necessary to remove one length, so cut it off as close as possible to the last crimp bead.

8 Treating the two wires remaining as one, attach one end of the necklace to one part of the clasp using a crimp bead (see Using Nylon-coated Wire with Crimp Beads, page 14). Trim the wire ends.

9 Using some of the wire trimmings, make three drops of different lengths by fixing a crimp bead to the end of each wire and thread on beads as required. Thread a crimp bead onto the three wires together and secure in place, then trim one wire as close as possible to the crimp bead, as in Step 7. Attach the two wires as one to the circle part of the toggle clasp, as in Step 8.

A little spell for the emotionally upset: place a piece of amethyst in the palm of your dominant hand, pour all your hurt feelings into the stone and then shout as you throw the stone away from you with as much force as possible. The hurt is supposed to disappear with the stone. Please, however, be careful where you do this!

Graceful Earrings

Time to make 15 minutes • **Ease of making** 3 • **Length** 6cm (2½in)

These beautiful drop earrings are very simply made following the instructions for Using Headpins and Multiple Headpins, pages 16–17, using the same teardrop beads as in the necklace, together with a few matching rocailles. The niobium ear-hooks look stunning and their purple anodized colouring is very durable. Niobium is a metal especially suitable for those with allergies to other metals.

One of the most spectacular members of the quartz family, amethyst displays a wide variety of quality and colour, from pale milky colours to the deep, dark purple gemstone seen here.

Aquamarine

Like emerald, aquamarine is a form of beryl, one of the oldest minerals prized by man, but unlike the best examples of its more regal cousin, this is a more affordable stone. Crystals of beryl can be found together with tourmaline, topaz, quartz and fluorite in pegmatites – a rich vein of mineral formed within cracks in granite rocks. These large and often very long crystals can sometimes grow to enormous sizes of up to 18m (59ft), but these large examples are usually of poorer quality.

In terms of reputed magical powers, aquamarine has different attributes to those of its richer relative emerald, and is considered to be a stone of courage and self-knowledge, which enables those who tend to be over-critical to temper their judgement with gentleness. It is also said that those who carry or wear aquamarine become more responsive to psychic happenings, as the conscious mind is opened to allow reception of spiritual impulses and clairvoyance. Aquamarine is also known for its ability to bring clarity of thought and perception, and thus aid the resolution of problems.

In the realm of health, aquamarine is believed to ease the pain of toothache as well as alleviate throat and jaw problems. It is also thought to be generally protective against illness and pollutants.

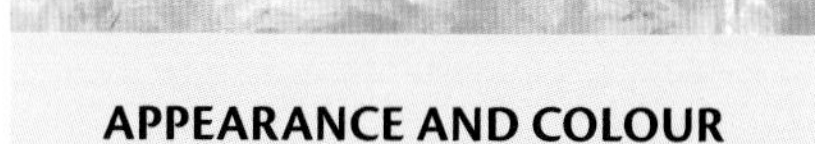

APPEARANCE AND COLOUR
Transparent, translucent or opaque in shades of pale blue/green

AVAILABILITY IN BEAD FORM
Easily available as tumble-chip beads; more rare and expensive in round or faceted beads

COUNTRIES OF ORIGIN
Afghanistan, Brazil, Columbia, India, Ireland, Mexico, Pakistan, Russia, Zimbabwe

BUYER'S GUIDE

Aquamarine is fairly easily available in bead form and the least expensive examples, such as tumble-chip beads, can be found at reasonable cost. However, beads with great clarity and attractive colour are expensive. Aquamarine-coloured glass can make a good substitute.

Evening Ocean

Time to make 1 hour • **Ease of making** 3 • **Length** 51cm (20in)

Have you ever watched the sun sink into the sea and later observed the silver aqua of the evening ocean? To my mind, the colour of clear aquamarine mirrors this natural beauty, and so here I have teamed the aquamarine beads with another watery item, the freshwater pearl.

In my first attempt at making this necklace I used 'silver' findings and beads, but after completing it I was dissatisfied with the look, as somehow the colour of the aquamarine had 'died'! So, I took it all apart and remade it with 'gold' accompaniments and am now much happier with the result. However, don't let that stop you using 'silver' if that is your preference, as all the beads and findings are available in both finishes.

This necklace was inexpensive to make because the aquamarine string is not of the best quality, but if you were to choose faceted and/or clearer aquamarine beads instead, you would expect to pay more.

To the uninitiated, this necklace might appear difficult to make, but rest assured that it is not! Simple stringing is all that is required, with no hidden difficulties to cause you problems.

Aquamarine makes the perfect gift between couples on their wedding day, as within the context of relationships it is considered to be a stone of joy, peace and happiness.

INGREDIENTS

- 40cm (16in) string of aquamarine cushion beads, 4mm thick
- 41 peacock-coloured freshwater pearls, 3mm
- 10 gold-plated fancy rondel beads, 5mm
- 79 gold-plated beaded rondel beads, 3mm
- 11 gold-plated faceted bicone beads, 3mm
- 16 aquamarine beads, 2–3mm (if difficult to obtain, use rocaille beads instead)
- 16 small aquamarine-coloured rocaille beads
- 3 goldfill beads, 2mm
- 3 gold-plated beads caps, 3mm
- 2 gold-plated 2–1 links
- 1 gold-plated rectangular pendant
- 1 gold-plated toggle clasp
- 12 goldfill crimp beads
- 9 x 8mm (⅜in) lengths of 'gold' gimp
- 25cm (10in) length of fine nylon-coated wire
- 3 x 20cm (8in) lengths of fine nylon-coated wire

In times long past, aquamarine was carried by sailors to protect them from drowning.

The Emperor Nero is believed to have had a monocle made from pale aquamarine to aid his short-sighted vision. For this reason, perhaps, the stone is now considered to be helpful to those with eyesight problems.

1 Using a goldfill crimp bead and one length of the gimp, attach one end of one of the 20cm (8in) lengths of nylon-coated wire to one part of the clasp (see Using Nylon-coated Wire with Gimp and Crimp Beads, page 15 – use this method for all the attachments). Thread the sequence of beads shown in the photograph on page 37 for one side of the necklace onto the wire and then attach the wire to the top loop of one of the 2–1 links.

2 Repeat Step 1 to make up the other side of the necklace.

3 Attach the remaining 20cm (8in) length of wire to the inside loop of one of the 2–1 links, then thread the sequence of beads shown in the photograph for the inner central strand. When all the beads are threaded, attach the wire to the corresponding loop of the other 2–1 link.

4 Repeat Step 3 with the remaining longer length of wire to make up the outer central strand, making sure to thread on the pendant in the centre of the strand.

5 In making up the main body of the necklace, you will have trimmed the spare wire. Apply a crimp bead to one end of three of these short lengths. Thread on the sequences of beads shown in the photograph to make three short, uneven drops for the back tassel.

6 Thread these three wires through the remaining crimp bead, then thread them through the remaining length of gimp. Attach the tassel to the circle of the clasp and thread the three lengths of wire back through the crimp bead (diagram A). Secure the crimp bead by squeezing it with pliers, then trim all the spare wire to complete the necklace.

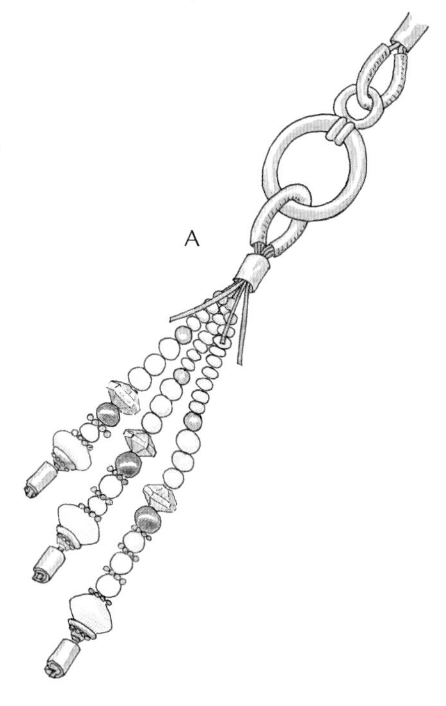

Ocean Drops

Time to make 15 minutes • **Ease of making** 3 • **Length** 5cm (2in)

Those who want the aquamarine look but not the expense might wish to consider using inexpensive glass beads, such as the faceted examples from the Czech Republic seen here. They have all the appeal of high-quality, clear and highly coloured aquamarine at a fraction of the cost.

For those without pierced ears I have used sterling silver ear-screws that clip neatly to the ear and are easily adjustable so that they fit without pinching. This type of ear-fitting can be used as an alternative for nearly all the other earrings in the book.

To make the earrings, simply use the photograph as a guide to threading and follow the instructions for Using Headpins, page 16, to make up and attach the beaded drops to the links and then attach the links to the ear-fittings.

INGREDIENTS

- 2 faceted aquamarine glass beads, 8mm
- 2 small aquamarine-coloured rocaille beads
- 2 silver-plated fancy links, 20mm
- 4 silver-plated bead caps, 3mm
- 2 silver-plated headpins
- 1 pair of sterling silver ear-screws

Crystal

Time to make 40 minutes • **Ease of making** 2 • **Length** 56cm (22in)

Aquamarine in the raw appears in the form of crystals, and the large beads seen here are as close to as their natural form as possible. I purchased these in the form of a small and roughly graduated bracelet, and not all the beads were suitable for use. If you have difficulty in finding crystal beads such as these, or they are too expensive, you could make a very similar necklace by substituting large tumble-chip beads (see Pair Drops below).

If you purchase a similar string, remove the beads from the thread and, after removing any unsuitable beads, re-graduate them (preferably in the groove of a beading tray), then use the photograph as a guide to threading and follow the instructions for Using Nylon-coated Wire with Crimp Beads, page 14. You will need to apply a crimp bead to either end of the threaded section so that the beads are held in position in the centre of the length of wire.

INGREDIENTS

- 18cm (7in) string of graduated aquamarine crystal beads
- 10 aquamarine beads, 4mm
- 60 aquamarine beads, 2–3mm
- 14 gold-plated thin rondel beads, 8mm
- 14 gold-plated thin rondel beads, 4mm
- 22 gold-plated plain rondel beads, 3mm
- 2 goldfill oval beads, 3 x 5mm
- 1 gold-plated toggle clasp
- 4 goldfill crimp beads
- 64cm (25in) length of 'gold' nylon-coated wire

Pair Drops

Time to make 30 minutes • **Ease of making** 3 • **Length** 6.5cm (2½in)

INGREDIENTS

- 4 aquamarine tumble-chip beads, about 9 x 7mm
- 8 round aquamarine beads, 4mm
- 4 gold-plated thin rondel beads, 8mm
- 4 gold-plated thin rondel beads, 4mm
- 4 goldfill oval beads, 3 x 5mm
- 6 goldfill crimp beads
- 1 pair of gold-plated fancy ear-studs
- 2 x 12.5cm (5in) lengths of 'gold' nylon-coated wire

These delicate earrings could be worn together with the Crystal necklace, but they look equally good on their own. As the large beads are tumble-chips, the earrings are not expensive to make.

To make them up, use the photograph as a guide to threading and follow the instructions for Using Nylon-coated Wire with Crimp Beads, pages 14 and 17.

Azurite & Malachite

Azurite and malachite are frequently found in symbiosis (see Exotica, opposite) and both are forms of carbonate of copper. Azurite was given its name by the Persians, who named it after the colour blue; think of azure skies and then it is easy to see how this stone became known as a 'stone of heaven'.

To many past civilizations, azurite became a stone worn by those of high standing. It was held sacred by the Native Americans and believed to enable direct, clear communication. Even today, azurite is considered to aid understanding, raise consciousness, enhance memory and relieve the emotional stress of anxiety or sadness. On the physical side of well-being, it is reputed to alleviate joint, spine and brain problems, as well as to help those suffering from problems of the liver, spleen, kidneys and thyroid.

Malachite is a brilliant green stone that is renowned for its powerful protective attributes. It is regarded as a stone that encourages risk- taking yet, conversely, it is also a stone for travellers, who are believed to be safe from physical dangers when wearing it. Gazing at the beautiful colour of malachite is soothing, while holding a piece in the hand is reputed to calm the emotions and confer peace. Sales people would do well to wear the stone at work, since it is regarded as a stone for promoting business, with better deals and transactions known to have been achieved in its presence!

As regards health, malachite is believed to aid childbirth and to support the immune system, in addition to alleviating asthma, arthritis and travel sickness, and lowering blood pressure.

APPEARANCE AND COLOUR
Opaque deep azure blue or deep green; often two colours combined together

AVAILABILITY IN BEAD FORM
Fairly common but moderately expensive

COUNTRIES OF ORIGIN
Australia, Chile, Egypt, England, France, Middle East, Namibia, Peru, Romania, Siberia, USA, Zambia

BUYER'S GUIDE

Azurite and malachite are both striking in appearance and relatively inexpensive. Both stones are fairly soft, so take care not to place your azurite/ malachite jewellery near to any material that may damage it.

Exotica

Time to make necklace 30 minutes; earrings 15 minutes • **Ease of making** necklace 2; earrings 3 • **Length** necklace 51cm (20in); earrings 5cm (2in)

Displaying the exuberant colours of both azurite and malachite, this vibrant necklace and earrings set uses most of the beads from a 40cm (16in) string – the remaining projects in this chapter offer ideas for using up the two leftover beads.

These beads are so lovely that I have kept the designs simple, which means that the items are some of the easiest in the book and can be tackled by a complete beginner to beaded jewellery making. In order to add extra interest to the earrings, I have used niobium ear-hooks that match the colour of the azurite beads.

To make the jewellery, use the photographs as a guide to threading and follow the instructions for Using Nylon-coated Wire with Gimp and Crimp Beads, page 15, for the necklace, and Using Headpins, page 16, for the earrings.

Azurite is one of the birthstones for Sagittarius.

NECKLACE INGREDIENTS

- 30 beads from a 40cm (16in) string of azurite beads, 12mm
- 20 gold-plated fancy rondel beads, 7mm
- 2 gold-plated fancy rondel beads, 4mm
- 20 gold-plated fancy rondel beads, 3mm
- 11 frosted teal-coloured large rocaille beads
- 2 goldfill crimp beads
- 1 gold-plated toggle clasp
- 2 x 8mm (⅜in) lengths of 'gold' gimp
- 60cm (24in) length of thick nylon-coated wire

EARRINGS INGREDIENTS

- 2 azurite beads, 12mm
- 6 frosted teal-coloured large rocaille beads
- 2 gold-plated fancy rondel beads, 6mm
- 2 gold-plated bead caps, 9mm
- 4 gold-plated bead caps, 3mm
- 4 goldfill oval beads, 3 x 5mm
- 2 goldfill headpins
- 1 pair of blue anodized niobium straight-leg ear-hooks

The beautiful blue of azurite has been much prized as a paint pigment for thousands of years and was used in the murals of ancient civilizations.

Triplet

Time to make 30 minutes • **Ease of making** 2 • **Length** 48cm (19in), plus 10cm (4in) drop

Triplet features a single azurite bead as the 'main event' in an inexpensive necklace. It is strung on waxed cotton cord, with the drops suspended on 'gold' nylon-coated wire.

INGREDIENTS

- ✧ 1 azurite bead, 12mm
- ✧ 3 frosted teal-coloured bugle beads, 10mm
- ✧ 35 frosted teal-coloured large rocaille beads
- ✧ 1 gold-plated fancy rondel bead, 7mm
- ✧ 3 gold-plated fancy cube beads, 6mm
- ✧ 8 gold-plated fancy rondel beads, 4mm
- ✧ 1 gold-plated thin rondel bead, 4mm
- ✧ 1 gold-plated cone-shaped bead cap, 9mm
- ✧ 6 gold-plated bead caps, 4mm
- ✧ 3 gold-plated pendant leaf drops, 8mm
- ✧ 1 gold-plated coin 3–1 link
- ✧ 3 goldfill oval beads, 3 x 5mm
- ✧ 1 gold-plated toggle clasp
- ✧ 8 goldfill crimp beads
- ✧ 2 gold-plated clamshell calottes
- ✧ 4 x 9cm (3½in) lengths of 'gold' nylon-coated wire
- ✧ 58cm (23in) length of black 1mm waxed cotton cord
- ✧ bottle of liquid superglue

1 Using the photograph as a guide to threading, make up the central pendant with its triple drops with the four lengths of nylon-coated wire, then make up the attachments to the leaf drops and the coin link (see Using Nylon-coated Wire with Crimp Beads, page 14). Leave an open loop at the top, above the cone-shaped bead cap, for threading onto the necklace.

2 Attach a clamshell calotte to one end of the waxed cotton cord, applying a tiny touch of superglue to the knot (see Using Beading Thread with Clamshell Calottes, page 15). Tie another overhand knot 18cm (7in) from the calotte (adjust this distance if you want to make your necklace longer or shorter). Thread on the rocaille and fancy rondel beads as shown, and after three sequences, thread through the top loop of the central drop and then continue threading on the remainder of the rocaille and fancy rondel beads.

3 Push all the threaded beads up together and then, leaving a little play in the cord, tie another overhand knot next to the last threaded bead. Leave a gap of 18cm (7in) before applying the second clamshell calotte, as in Step 2.

4 Finish by attaching the clasp to the calottes by opening and closing the calotte loops sideways.

Solo

Time to make 10 minutes • **Ease of making** 3 • **Length** 46cm (18in), plus 5cm (2in) drop

Again featuring a single azurite bead, this necklace has a simple drop hanging from a sterling silver chain. It is made using the technique to form an earring drop in Using Headpins, page 16.

INGREDIENTS

- ✧ 1 azurite bead, 12mm
- ✧ 1 teal-coloured large rocaille bead
- ✧ 1 silver-plated cone-shaped bead cap, 9mm
- ✧ 1 silver-plated bead cap, 6mm
- ✧ 1 silver-plated small pendant
- ✧ 1 silver-plated bail
- ✧ 1 silver-plated headpin
- ✧ 46cm (18in) length of sterling silver chain

Circlets

Time to make 30 minutes • **Ease of making** 3 • **Length** 5cm (2in)

INGREDIENTS

- ✧ 10 malachite beads, 4mm
- ✧ 12 silver-plated faceted bicone beads, 3mm
- ✧ 14 green small rocaille beads
- ✧ 10 silver-plated bead caps, 3mm
- ✧ 2 silver-plated 5-hole pendant drops
- ✧ 12 silver-plated headpins
- ✧ 1 pair of fancy ear-studs
- ✧ 1 pair of clutch-backs for ear-studs

Beautiful silver-plated pewter findings give these earrings a professionally made look, which is enhanced by the gorgeous deep green of the 4mm malachite beads and tiny rocailles.

They look difficult to make, but any beginner who has mastered the art of forming loops in wire can tackle this project with ease. Follow the instructions for Using Headpins and Multiple Headpins, pages 16–17, and use the photograph as a guide to threading.

Rainforest

Time to make 30 minutes • **Ease of making** 2 • **Length** 43cm (17in)

INGREDIENTS

- ✧ 40cm (16in) string of malachite beads, 4mm
- ✧ 1 malachite tapered set
- ✧ 1 vermeil Chinese-style clasp
- ✧ 2 goldfill crimp beads
- ✧ 2 x 8mm (⅜in) lengths of 'gold' gimp
- ✧ 51cm (20in) length of nylon-coated wire

Rainforest is a simple-to-make yet supremely elegant necklace that sits closely to the neck, and therefore the heart, where malachite's reputed ability to attract and enhance love is said to be strongest.

The drops are purchased in ready-made tapered sets and are as simply strung as any other bead. However, it is important when making this necklace to leave enough play in the threading material for the drops to swing freely, otherwise they will not hang correctly.

To make the necklace, use the photograph as a guide to threading and follow the instructions for Using Nylon-coated Wire with Gimp and Crimp Beads, page 15.

Malachite and azurite combine together with powerful force to bring emotional healing, psychic vision and help in alleviating muscle cramps.

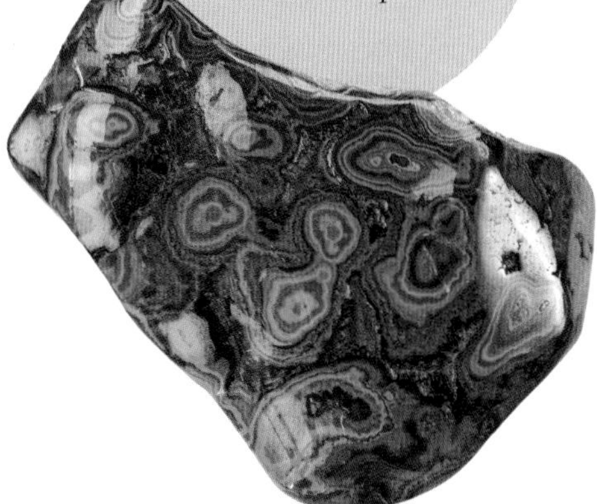

Blue Lace Agate

Blue lace agate has a beautiful, delicate appearance that is so at odds with the more earthy shades of other agates that it is difficult to believe they are the same type of stone. It is also a little less commonly found than the duller shades of agate and therefore slightly more expensive.

It is perhaps not surprising that a stone with such a wonderful soft blue colour should be regarded as cooling and soothing to both mind and body, and therefore have a reputed ability to calm anger and emotional stress. Among its other attributes, blue lace agate is believed to aid verbal expression of thoughts and emotions and to give release from feelings of repression or rejection.

Renowned as a gentle healing stone, it is considered effective against infection, inflammation and throat problems. It is also thought to be helpful in the treatment of skeletal problems such as fractures and arthritis.

To benefit from the many powers of blue lace agate, it should be worn at the throat, while holding it in the hand is said to be the best way to dispel anger.

APPEARANCE AND COLOUR
Opaque or translucent, usually in soft wavy bands of pale blue

AVAILABILITY IN BEAD FORM
Relatively common

COUNTRIES OF ORIGIN
Most parts of the world, especially Africa, Brazil, Czech Republic, India, Morocco, USA

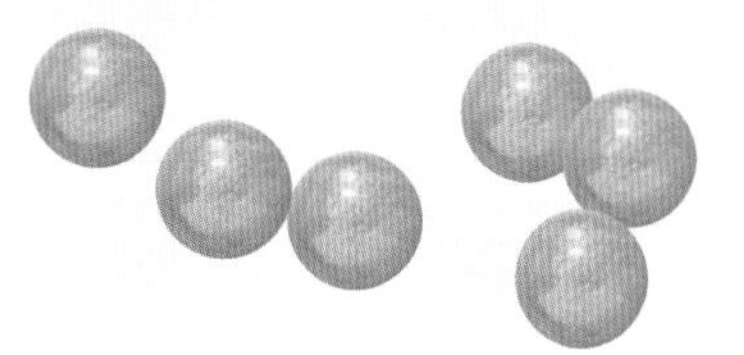

BUYER'S GUIDE

These pretty stones are easily available in many shapes and sizes at a relatively low price. Larger beads like the oval one below often exhibit the delicate lace effect. Some of the smaller and more plain blue lace agate beads may be colour-enhanced, but the more lacy stone would be spoilt by such treatment.

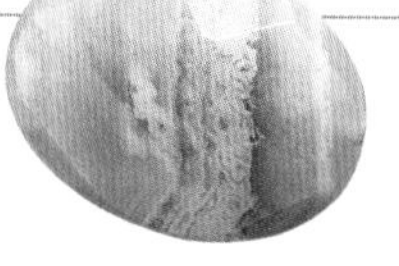

Baby Blue

Time to make 30 minutes • **Ease of making** 3 • **Length** 41cm (16in)

Because of its gorgeous colour and special attributes for men, Baby Blue would make a perfect gift for the mother of a newborn baby boy. Being a choker, it is worn at the throat, where its powers are said to be strongest.

The necklace is simple to make and is 'strung' on memory wire. This is a special wire that 'remembers' its shape, so that after opening to put on, it simply returns to its coiled form to close and sits snugly against the neck without the need for a clasp. The cut ends of this wire are very sharp; consequently, it is important to either fold these over completely, as here, or to fit special beads over the ends to prevent injury.

After making this necklace, you will have nine large and six small blue lace agate beads left over. These could be used in another necklace, or to make a coordinating bracelet or several pairs of earrings.

INGREDIENTS

- 15 rectangular faceted blue lace agate beads, from a 40cm (16in) string, 15 x 10mm
- 19 blue lace agate beads, from a power bracelet, 8mm
- 35 silver-plated fancy rondel beads, 4mm
- 4 silver-plated headpins
- 3 silver-plated jump rings
- 1½ coils of necklace-length memory wire

1 Make up the three drops and attach them to the jump rings by using the photograph as a guide for threading and following the instructions for Using Headpins, page 16.

2 With a strong pair of pliers, grasp the tip of one end of the wire and bend it over. Keep bending and then squeeze in place so that it appears as in diagram A. This will take some force, as the wire is very resistant to bending.

3 Thread on the beads in the sequence shown in the photograph, leaving a little 'play' in the wire to allow the beads to move. Repeat Step 2 with the other end of the wire to complete the necklace.

A

In the home, a piece of blue lace agate placed in a dish and surrounded by the light from pale blue candles is reputed to dispel family quarrels.

Blue lace agate could be regarded as an ideal stone to give to a baby boy; first of all for its soft blue colour and secondly because it is said to help enhance the sensitive and caring aspects of a man's nature.

Puffed Hearts

Time to make 30 minutes• **Ease of making** 3 • **Length** 6cm (2½in)

These elegant earrings swing with free movement on sterling silver figaro chain. They look expensive but are made at very reasonable cost. The beads are taken from a 40cm (16in) string and enough will be left over to make a matching necklace or bracelet. Make them up using the photograph as a guide to threading and following the instructions for Using Headpins, page 16.

INGREDIENTS

- ✧ 6 blue lace agate hearts, 8mm
- ✧ 6 sterling silver jump rings, 4mm
- ✧ 6 sterling silver headpins, 25mm (if available, to save on cost)
- ✧ 1 pair of silver-plated ear-studs with holes for 3 drops
- ✧ 1 pair of silver-plated clutch-backs for ear-studs
- ✧ 20cm (8in) length of sterling silver figaro chain

Blue Jeans

Time to make 30 minutes • **Ease of making** 2 • **Length** 48cm (19in)

This easy-to-make necklace is a delightful item that will especially appeal to the young. It is one of the least expensive items in the book and the design is suitable for use with other stone types – rose quartz, rock crystal, aventurine and so on are available in this form. It would be an ideal candidate for money-making ventures, such as craft markets and fairs.

INGREDIENTS

- ✧ 1 blue lace agate tumble-stone with hole drilled across the top, about 30 x 18mm
- ✧ 1 silver-plated hook clasp
- ✧ 2 silver-plated box calottes
- ✧ 3 x 76cm (30in) lengths of faux suede, 1 white, 1 pale blue, 1 mid-blue

1 Secure one of the box calottes to one end of all three lengths of faux suede to hold them all securely together (see Using Thong or Cord with Box Calottes and Jump Rings, page 16).

2 Plait (braid) the three lengths of faux suede for a length of 23cm (9in), as far as the centre of the necklace, then thread the tumble-stone onto one of the lengths of faux suede. Carry on plaiting (braiding) until the two sides of the necklace match and then secure the remaining box calotte over the lengths of faux suede, as in Step 1. At this point, the lengths may not match, so use a sharp knife or pair of cutting pliers to trim the excess. Attach the hook clasp to one of the box calottes to complete.

Blue lace agate is one of the birthstones for Pisces.

Multi Tassel

Time to make 3 hours • **Ease of making** 4 • **Length** 86cm (34in), including tassel

To the natural stone novice, the large blue beads seen here look very similar to blue lace agate, but they are in fact dyed onyx – a variety of agate that lends itself well to the dying process. It is often seen in blue, as here, or in green, as on page 23. The smallest blue beads are blue lace agate.

This necklace, which could be made with many different types of bead, looks complicated, but in fact a beginner could tackle it with ease. The ingredients list only gives a range for the size of the main beads to avoid unnecessary complication.

To make the necklace, use the photograph as a guide to threading and follow the instructions for Using Nylon-coated Wire with Gimp and Crimp Beads, page 15, and Using Thong or Cord with Box Calottes and Jump Rings, page 16. However, don't try to copy the design exactly. Simply thread beads onto short, random lengths of nylon-coated wire and attach them to the box calottes at the ends of five mixed lengths of faux suede, then attach the toggle clasp. Make up the tassel in the same way with the remaining two lengths of faux suede and lengths of silver chain, then suspend all the drops from a large jump ring before attaching to the circle of the toggle clasp.

INGREDIENTS

- ✧ 38 silver-plated beads, 4–17mm
- ✧ 38 natural stone beads, 4–15mm
- ✧ 16 peacock-coloured freshwater pearls, 3mm
- ✧ 20 blue rocaille beads
- ✧ 1 blue fancy glass bead
- ✧ 2 silver-plated small pendants
- ✧ 3 silver-plated bead caps
- ✧ 1 silver-plated toggle clasp
- ✧ 14 silver-plated box calottes
- ✧ 25 sterling silver crimp beads
- ✧ 1 silver-plated jump ring
- ✧ 20 x 8mm (⅜in) lengths of 'silver' gimp
- ✧ 61cm (24in) length of nylon-coated wire, cut into 13 uneven lengths
- ✧ 30cm (12in) length of blue faux suede, cut into 4 uneven lengths
- ✧ 21cm (8¼in) length of grey faux suede, cut into 3 uneven lengths
- ✧ 24cm (9½in) length of sterling silver chain, cut into 3 uneven lengths

Carnelian Agate

'Carnelian is a talisman, It brings good luck to child and man. It drives away all evil things; To thee and thine protection brings. From such a gem a woman gains sweet hope and comfort in her pains.'

This extract from an 18th-century poem by Goethe sums up many of the mystical attributes of carnelian. Few stones have been held in such widespread regard for so long.

As early as 2500 BC, the Egyptians wore carnelian in the belief that it would bring peace by dispelling envy, anger and hatred. Even today, carnelian is considered to hold special powers. It is particularly prized in Western Asia, as the Prophet Mohammed wore a carnelian set into a silver seal ring. The people of Turkmenistan believe that a piece of carnelian tied around a baby's neck will protect the baby's sight and bring good health. This connection with health-enhancing properties may have arisen from the blood red colour of some carnelian stones.

Carnelian is also reputed to promote courage, eloquence and self-confidence, as well as protect the home from lightning. One of its more unlikely qualities is a supposed power to save its wearer from falling walls. A 17th-century writer states: *'No man who wore a carnelian was ever found in a collapsed house or under a fallen wall.'*

APPEARANCE AND COLOUR
Translucent to clear mixtures of white, gold, reddish amber, grey and brown

AVAILABILITY IN BEAD FORM
Common in both natural and dyed colours

COUNTRIES OF ORIGIN
Africa, Brazil, Czech Republic, India, Morocco, USA

BUYER'S GUIDE

The best carnelian is a clear, deep amber colour. Poorer stone is sometimes dyed to masquerade as that of a superior quality. A reputable supplier will tell you if the colour is enhanced. Carnelian is generally an inexpensive stone, but some faceted and transparent beads can be more costly.

The Rough with the Smooth

Time to make 45 minutes • **Ease of making** 3 • **Length** 58cm (23in)

Delightfully rough stones such as these are not commonplace, but if you like this look, they are worth seeking out. These examples were very inexpensive, but the finished necklace would be sure to command a hefty price tag in a high street store.

The rough stones are as they were found, and the simple addition of holes has turned the raw material into beads that can only improve as they age and develop a patina. As a foil to their primitive charms, I have added some polished carnelian from India and a small touch of 'gold' in the clasp and 3–1 necklace ends. The necklace is simple and quick to make, and strung with thick nylon-covered wire because it is fairly heavy.

INGREDIENTS

- 2 x 40cm (16in) strings of rough carnelian beads, 15–18mm
- 3 polished barrel carnelian beads, 20 x 9mm
- 2 polished barrel carnelian beads, 15 x 8mm
- 10 polished round carnelian beads, 8mm
- 1 gold-plated fancy washer bead
- 2 gold-plated 3–1 necklace ends
- 1 gold-plated toggle clasp
- 10 goldfill crimp beads
- 1.35m (1.5yd) length of thick nylon-coated wire

1 Cut the length of wire into five lengths: 3 x 25cm (10in) and 2 x 30cm (12in).

2 Using a crimp bead, attach one end of one of the 25cm (10in) lengths of wire to one part of the clasp (see Using Nylon-coated Wire with Crimp Beads, page 14).

3 Using the photograph as a guide, thread on beads in the sequence shown, then attach the free end of the wire to the single loop of one 3–1 necklace end, as in Step 2.

TIP
Many Indian semi-precious stone beads have less than perfect holes, so they can be difficult to thread. Use a bead reamer (see page 13) to enlarge the holes.

4 Repeat with another 25cm (10in) length of wire, attaching one end to the remaining part of the clasp and the other to the remaining 3–1 necklace end.

5 Attach the remaining 25cm (10in) length of wire to the inner loop of the three loops of one of the 3–1 necklace ends, as before.

6 Using the photograph of the necklace on page 49 as a guide, thread on beads in the sequence shown to make the inner strand of the necklace.

7 Make sure that the beads do not hang stiffly, i.e. that the wire is not pulled too tight, before attaching the end of the wire to the inner loop of the other 3–1 necklace end.

8 Repeat Steps 5–7 with the remaining two lengths of wire to thread the central and outer strands of the necklace.

Carnelian beads are to be found in many guises, from the delicate floral beads of the Lily Drops earrings below, to 40mm beads with etched surfaces, such as the rat-decorated Chinese bead seen in the necklace on page 8.

Lily Drops

Time to make 30 minutes • **Ease of making** 3 • **Length** 6cm (2½in)

The two lily-shaped carnelian beads used for these earrings are taken from a long string of 48 beads, which display to great effect carnelian's widely ranging hues. The beautifully carved and highly polished beads lend themselves perfectly to this style of drop earring, and the remaining beads provide material for many more in a variety of colours. The string of beads is relatively expensive, but proves to be very good value when making earrings – and no two pairs will be exactly the same.

INGREDIENTS

- ✧ 2 flower-shaped carnelian beads
- ✧ 10 'gold' lustred rocaille beads
- ✧ 2 gold-plated plain washer beads
- ✧ 2 oval goldfill beads, 3 x 5mm
- ✧ 8 goldfill beads, 2mm
- ✧ 8 goldfill headpins
- ✧ 1 pair of straight-leg goldfill ear-hooks

1 Make up the ear-hooks, threading on a 2mm goldfill bead and a rocaille onto each 'leg' (see Step 6 of Using Headpins, page 16).

2 Trim the pin end of one headpin. Make a loop in one end of the trimmed headpin (see Using Headpins, page 16), and thread on a flower-shaped bead followed by a washer bead, a rocaille bead and an oval goldfill bead.

3 Trim the spare headpin wire to leave about 8mm (⅜in), then make another loop in the wire as before, as close to the threaded beads as possible.

4 Attach the loop just made to the loop of an ear-hook by opening and closing the latter sideways.

5 Trim the three remaining headpins to 1.8cm (¾in), 2.5cm (1in) and 3.5cm (1⅜in) in length. Thread each trimmed headpin with a rocaille bead and a 2mm goldfill bead.

6 Make a loop in the end of each trimmed headpin as before and attach to the wire loop at the bottom end of the flower-shaped bead before closing the loops. I have kept the longest wire in the centre of the three drops, but this is purely personal preference.

7 Repeat Steps 2–6 to make the second earring in the same way.

Carnelian is a hard stone that does not chip easily, and for this reason you may be lucky and find inexpensive old beads, such as those pictured here, in places like the dusty souks of the Middle East.

About Face

Time to make 1 hour • **Ease of making** 5 • **Length** 66cm (26in)

Carnelian lends itself especially to carving techniques and therefore beads with decorated surfaces are often to be found. One side of these Chinese 'face' beads has a polished Buddha-type face on a frosted-finish background, with, on the other side, leaves and Chinese lettering (leaving me once again wishing I could read it!)

With such ornate beads, it seems best to choose an uncluttered design and let the beads speak for themselves. Therefore, this simple necklace has no additional beads and is strung on three strands of plain waxed cotton cord, which is plaited (braided) at either end. As the finished necklace is long, it will simply slip over the head, so I have not used a clasp but have attached the two ends together with a 'silver' open heart connector. If you wish to make the necklace shorter, you will need to add a clasp.

TIP
You may wish to use one colour of waxed cotton cord instead of two contrasting colours, such as the natural and brown featured here.

INGREDIENTS

- 40cm (16in) string of carnelian beads, 20mm
- 1 'silver' open heart or other connector
- 2 silver-plated box calottes
- 2 silver-plated jump rings
- 2 x 1.5m (1.7yd) lengths of 1mm waxed cotton cord in 2 contrasting colours
- 4 x 30cm (12in) lengths of 1mm waxed cotton cord in 2 contrasting colours

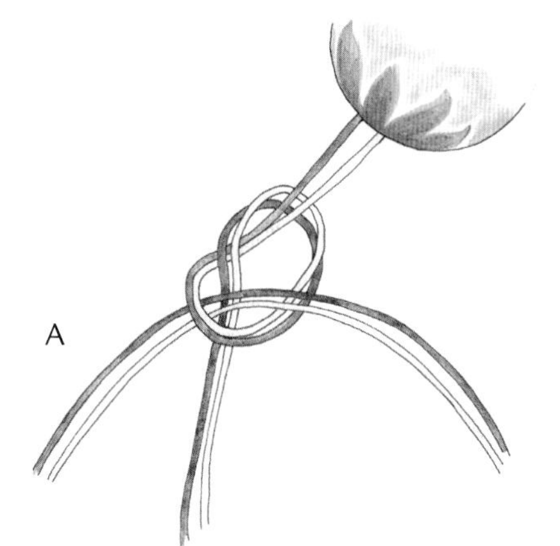

TIP
Giving carnelian to a woman friend? Why not incorporate the following old saying in a gift tag note: *'She loving once and always, wears if wise, carnelian – and her home is paradise.'*

1 Before starting, make sure that two strands of waxed cotton cord will pass through each of the beads. Tie the two 1.5m (1.7yd) lengths of cord together 20cm (8in) from one end using a loose overhand knot.

2 Thread one bead onto the two threads together – any smaller ones should be used at either end of the necklace. After threading, tie an overhand knot in the two threads together as close to the bead as possible.

3 Repeat Step 2 until all the beads are threaded and knotted, then tie a loose overhand knot in the two threads together after the last bead.

4 Pass two of the 30cm (12in) lengths of waxed cotton cord halfway through the first loose knot and the remaining two halfway through the last loose knot (diagram A).

5 Tighten the loose knot against the first bead and then plait (braid) the six strands together in pairs, keeping contrasting colours of waxed cotton cord together. Plait (braid) a length of 9cm (3½in) (or to suit yourself), then trim any spare thread and apply a box calotte to cover the cut ends (see Using Thong or Cord with Box Calottes and Jump Rings, page 16).

6 Using a jump ring, attach the box calotte to one part of the open heart or other connector (see Using Thong or Cord with Box Calottes and Jump Rings, page 16).

7 Repeat Steps 5–6 to complete the other end of the necklace.

Citrine & Smoky Quartz

The golden glowing colour of some citrine explains its reputation for holding the power of the sun, and also the belief that it is a warming and energizing stone that dispels negativity and promotes creativity, abundance and prosperity. Harmony is another positive power ascribed to citrine – discord in families and other social groups is said to dissipate in its presence! In promoting good health, citrine is reputed to be cleansing, stimulating, beneficial to the digestion and circulation, and also to improve the eyesight.

For jewellery makers it is a beautiful stone, with a clarity exhibited by only a few others, which makes it useful for dressy styles. Known as a stone of abundance and sometimes called 'the merchant's stone', those who hope to sell their jewellery may like to keep a piece of citrine, as placing it in a cash box is reputed to attract money and help hold on to it.

Smoky quartz is a colour variation of citrine, but is often referred to and regarded as a separate stone. The colour is less striking, but nonetheless beautiful, and appears in various shades ranging from clear pale to dark brown.

APPEARANCE AND COLOUR
Clear crystal clusters or inside geodes (hollow stones) in shades of yellow, amber and smoky brown

AVAILABILITY IN BEAD FORM
Relatively uncommon and moderately priced

COUNTRIES OF ORIGIN
Brazil, France, Madagascar, UK (especially Scotland), USA

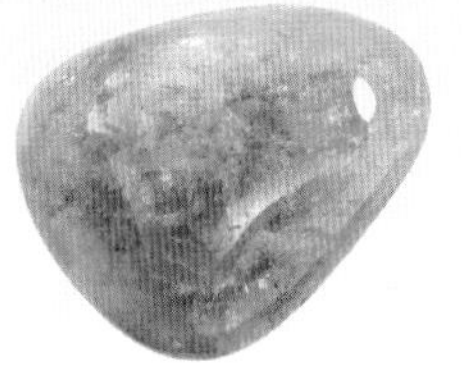

BUYER'S GUIDE

Citrine/smoky quartz is often found in faceted bead form. If you like the look but not the price, there are some very excellent look-alikes made from Czech glass.

Double Loop

Time to make 2 hours • **Ease of making** 3 • **Length** 102cm (40in)

The beads used here are a combination of smoky quartz and faceted Czech crystal glass beads. It would be possible to make the necklace entirely from smoky quartz, but while incorporating the glass beads does not detract from the stylish look, it does bring down the overall cost to make this an inexpensive item. If you buy a whole string of smoky quartz, you will have plenty left over for a matching bracelet and pair of earrings.

This design is easy to make and also offers maximum versatility, as it can be worn double with the clasp at the front, as a long, flapper style or single but knotted.

INGREDIENTS

- 6 faceted smoky quartz beads, 10mm
- 292 faceted Czech crystal glass beads, 3mm
- 2 silver-plated fancy rondel beads, 5mm
- 4 silver-plated fancy thin rondel beads, 4mm
- 12 silver-plated faceted bicone beads, 3mm
- 3 silver-plated cone-shaped bead caps, 10mm
- 1 silver-plated bead cap, 8mm
- 1 silver-plated toggle clasp
- 5 sterling silver headpins
- 4 sterling silver crimp beads
- 3 x 8mm (⅜in) lengths of 'silver' gimp
- 2 lengths of nylon-coated wire, 110cm (43in), 7cm (3in)
- 2 lengths of sterling silver fine rope chain, 15cm (6in), 5cm (2in)
- 3 lengths of sterling silver fine curb chain, 10cm (4in), 6cm (2½in), 3cm (1¼in)
- 2 lengths of sterling silver fine belcher chain, 6cm (2½in), 3cm (1¼in)

1 Using gimp and a crimp bead, attach one end of the long length of nylon-coated wire to one part of the clasp (see Using Nylon-coated Wire with Gimp and Crimp Beads, page 15). Thread one faceted glass bead, one 5mm rondel bead, one faceted glass bead and three faceted bicone beads onto the wire. Thread on 41 faceted glass beads followed by one faceted bicone bead, then thread through the end loop of the 15cm (6in) rope chain. Thread on another faceted bicone bead followed by the end loop of the 10cm (4in) curb chain, then thread on one more faceted bicone bead.

Citrine is sometimes known as a stone of joy and self-esteem, and is thought to promote pleasure in new experiences.

TIP
You can make this style of necklace from virtually any other bead combination, from wood to ruby!

2 Using the photograph as a guide, thread on the central bead sequence with cone-shaped bead caps at either end, then repeat Step 1 in reverse order to complete the main part of the necklace.

3 To make the tassel, thread one crimp bead and the end loop of each of the remaining silver chains onto the 7cm (3in) length of nylon-coated wire. Thread the wire back through the crimp bead to make a small loop at one end of the wire (diagram A). Secure the crimp bead in place with pliers, preferably crimp pliers.

4 Thread a faceted glass bead onto each headpin, form a loop in each and attach to the end of each length of chain (see Using Headpins, page 16).

5 Thread beads and bead caps onto the wire as shown in the photograph, then using the remaining crimp bead and gimp, attach the tassel to the circle part of the clasp, as in Step 1.

Sunshine

Time to make 1½ hours
• **Ease of making** 3
• **Length** 48cm (19in)

This necklace and earrings set incorporates three different styles of citrine beads: smooth rounds, faceted discs and baroque faceted chunks. They are all of a beautiful, delicate yellow hue and the round and faceted beads are so clear that they could be glass, so if you are looking to save money, you could substitute glass beads for these with little detriment to the end result. When made entirely from citrine beads, the cost is relatively high, but you will have many beads left over with which to make other jewellery items.

Normally, the clasp of a necklace is worn at the back of the necklace, but here, as in Double Loop (see page 53), it is made to be seen and therefore can be worn at the front of the neck as well as the back.

The earrings are simply made using some of the same beads as specified for the necklace, and referring to the photograph as a guide to threading and the instructions for Using Headpins, page 16.

INGREDIENTS

- ✧ 40cm (16in) string of citrine beads, 8mm
- ✧ 40cm (16in) string of faceted disc citrine beads, 7–8mm
- ✧ 40cm (16in) string of baroque faceted citrine beads, about 12 x 15mm
- ✧ 19 gold-plated beaded rondel beads, 7mm
- ✧ 1 gold-plated fancy flat disc, 7mm
- ✧ 5 gold-plated bead caps, 4mm
- ✧ a few pale 'gold' small rocaille beads
- ✧ 1 gold-plated toggle clasp
- ✧ 3 goldfill headpins
- ✧ 2 goldfill crimp beads
- ✧ 4 x 8mm (⅜in) lengths of 'gold' gimp
- ✧ 2 x 58cm (23in) lengths of nylon-coated wire

1 Using two lengths of gimp and a crimp bead, attach one end of the two lengths of nylon-coated wire to one part of the clasp (diagram A) (see Using Nylon-coated Wire with Gimp and Crimp Beads, page 15). Thread one bead cap and one rondel bead onto the two wires together.

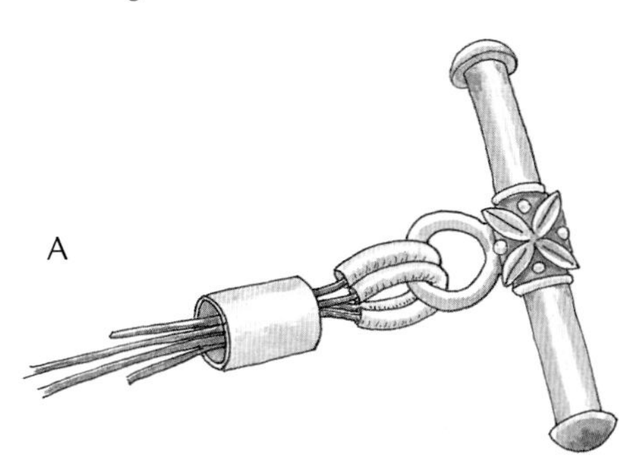

2 Thread three rocaille beads followed by the round and disc citrine bead sequence as shown in the photograph onto each length of wire. Then thread three more rocaille beads onto each wire (diagram B).

B

3 Thread both lengths of wire together through one rondel bead, one baroque citrine bead and then another rondel bead.

4 Repeat Steps 2–3 six more times. Repeat Steps 1–2 in reverse to complete the main threading and attach the necklace to the other part of the clasp.

5 Make the three-drop tassel using the photograph as a guide to threading and following the instructions for Using Headpins, page 16, then attach to the circle part of the clasp to complete the necklace.

The rare Scottish form of citrine is known as a Cairngorm, after the mountains where it is found. Gem-quality stones such as these are cut and polished for setting in gold or silver jewellery.

Place a piece of citrine in the far left (from the front door) corner of your house to bring prosperity to the household.

Crystal Quartz

Of all the natural stones, rock crystal or quartz must be the one most strongly associated with magical attributes – we are all familiar with the crystal ball, into which the scryer or fortune-teller looks to see what the future holds. It is also believed to be the best stone for all types of healing. Wearing the stone is said to relieve headache, while holding it in the hand is believed to reduce fever.

Worldwide, this rather spectacular and yet common stone has been revered and treasured for thousands of years. Today, most people simply purchase the stone for its sparkling beauty, and in bead form it is available in many different shapes. Recent additions to the bead jeweller's palette are the crackle quartz beads featured opposite. The dyed versions of these beads have an artificial appearance, but are very attractive nonetheless and ideal for creating jewellery that is delicate in style.

Rock crystal has a special association with the moon, and its magical powers are said to increase if it is left in the light of a full moon.

The Herkimer diamond pictured below is a special form of quartz that has a reputation for enhancing psychic powers. It is expensive and is not obtainable in bead form, but it is a beautiful crystal with especially good light-reflecting qualities.

APPEARANCE AND COLOUR
Transparent or milky, usually in clusters but sometimes single points; colourless

AVAILABILITY IN BEAD FORM
Common

COUNTRIES OF ORIGIN
Found worldwide

BUYER'S GUIDE

Rock crystal is usually brilliantly clear, and simple polishing reveals a beautiful sheen, while faceting releases the sparkle. The price of faceted quartz crystal beads is moderate, similar to that of Austrian crystal glass beads. Czech faceted glass beads are cheaper but less bright.

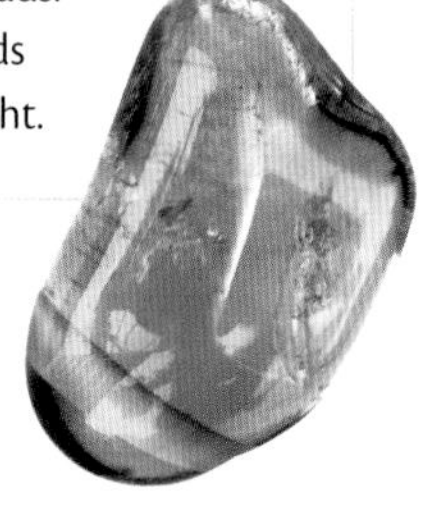

Crackle Quartz Collection

Time to make bracelets 1 hour/20 minutes; pendant 15 minutes
• **Ease of making** 3 • **Length** bracelets 20cm (8in); pendant 46cm (18n)

Newcomers to beading with semi-precious stone may find themselves daunted by the prospect of purchasing whole strings of beads rather than just the number required for a project, so here I show you how you can use all the beads down to the very last one! The main project is a beaded drop bracelet, and after making this, I was left with just six beads, five of which I put into another style of bracelet, with the remaining one becoming a stylish pendant on a rat-tail cord.

The featured beads are faceted artificially crackled quartz, and are both inexpensive and easily available. They are also often found in dyed pastel colours, but note that this dyed colour is unstable and could easily disappear, especially if the beads are left in the light.

The only skill needed to make the bracelets is forming loops in wire, so follow the instructions for Using Headpins and Multiple Headpins, pages 16–17, and use the photographs as a guide to threading. The same technique is required for the pendant drop necklace, but you also need to attach a clasp to the cord, so refer to the instructions for Using Thong or Cord with Box Calottes and Jump Rings, page 16.

BRACELETS AND PENDANT INGREDIENTS

- 40cm (16in) string of faceted oval crackled quartz beads, 18 x 15mm
- 27 gold-plated plain rondel beads, 3mm
- a few clear rocaille beads
- 2 gold-plated pendant drops
- 1 gold-plated bead cap, 3mm
- 1 gold-plated bail
- 1 gold-plated heart link clasp
- 1 gold-plated trigger clasp
- 1 gold-plated hook clasp
- 24 gold-plated headpins
- 2 gold-plated box calottes
- 18 gold-plated jump rings
- 20cm (8in) length of gold-plated curb chain, medium (5mm)
- 10cm (4in) length of gold-plated curb chain, large (7mm), cut into six 2-link pieces
- 46cm (18in) length of black rat-tail

An ideal place to keep a leftover quartz bead would be beneath your pillow, since doing so is said to induce peaceful sleep and psychic dreams!

'Diamond' Chandeliers

Time to make 20 minutes • **Ease of making** 3 • **Length** 4.5cm (1¾in)

Man's long fascination with the beauty of natural quartz crystal points may well have led to the style of crystal glass drops that is often seen in a crystal chandelier.

I am sure we would all love to be able to make diamond earrings, but I have yet to see beads made from diamonds, and besides, just think of the cost and the waste of drilling holes in such a precious stone! So for those with hankerings for the real thing, these sparkling quartz/crystal glass drops may satisfy your desire. To make the earrings, use the photograph as a guide to threading and follow the instructions for Using Headpins, page 16.

INGREDIENTS

- 2 faceted quartz beads, 8 x 6mm
- 6 faceted quartz beads, 4 x 3mm
- 4 Swarovski crystal beads, 4mm
- 8 Swarovski crystal bicone beads, 3mm
- 2 goldfill oval beads, 5 x 3mm
- 16 gold-plated plain rondel beads, 3mm
- 14 goldfill beads, 2mm
- 2 gold-plated 4-hole links
- 6 goldfill headpins
- 1 pair of goldfill ear-hooks

Titania

Time to make necklace 90 minutes; earrings 20 minutes • **Ease of making** necklace 5; earrings 3 • **Length** necklace 53cm (21in); earrings 7cm (3in)

This wonderful set of jewellery is made using clear quartz beads that have been treated with titanium tetrachloride in a process that produces an amazing iridescence. The rainbow effect is said to promote energy and enthusiasm for life, as well as bring peace to troubled relationships.

The necklace is knotted to give it fluidity, and I have chosen blue thread, but almost any would be suitable, as the beads exhibit such a wide range of beautiful hues. I have, however, only knotted between each of the quartz beads, leaving the rondel and glass crystal bead sections plainly strung, which halves the time involved and also saves on thread.

To make the earrings, use the photograph as a guide to threading and follow the instructions for Using Headpins, page 16. The findings are mainly goldfill, but I have also incorporated some blue anodized niobium headpins to match the thread of the necklace.

NECKLACE INGREDIENTS

- ✧ 40cm (16in) string of titanium quartz beads, 8mm
- ✧ 30 gold-plated fancy flat rondel beads, 4mm
- ✧ 15 AB-coated faceted Swarovski crystal beads, 4mm
- ✧ 1 gold-plated toggle clasp
- ✧ 2 x 8mm (⅜in) lengths of 'gold' gimp
- ✧ 84cm (33in) length of blue beading thread or silk beading thread with a needle attached
- ✧ bottle of liquid superglue (optional)

TIP
Be careful when handling superglue not to get any on your skin or on your beads!

EARRINGS INGREDIENTS

- ✧ 2 titanium quartz beads from the necklace string, 8mm
- ✧ 4 AB-coated faceted Swarovski crystal beads, 4mm
- ✧ 6 AB-coated Swarovski crystal bicone beads, 3mm
- ✧ 4 gold-plated fancy flat rondel beads, 4mm
- ✧ 8 gold-plated fancy rondel beads, 3mm
- ✧ 2 oval goldfill beads, 3 x 5mm
- ✧ 10 plain goldfill beads, 2mm
- ✧ 2 goldfill headpins
- ✧ 4 blue anodized niobium headpins
- ✧ 1 pair of straight-leg goldfill ear-hooks

1 Stiffen the length of beading thread with superglue (see page 15). Alternatively, you could use silk thread that already comes with a needle attached.

2 Thread one quartz bead onto the beading thread followed by one of the lengths of gimp, then thread through the loop of the clasp and back through the first quartz bead. Using the short length of thread, tie an overhand knot around the long length (diagram A). Using a headpin, very carefully apply a very tiny amount of superglue to seal this knot, then trim any spare thread close to the knot. The resulting knot should be large enough so that the beads will not slide over it, but if they do, you should start again with either a thicker or doubled length of thread.

A

3 Thread on the next quartz bead and then follow diagrams B–F to make the next knot in the thread.

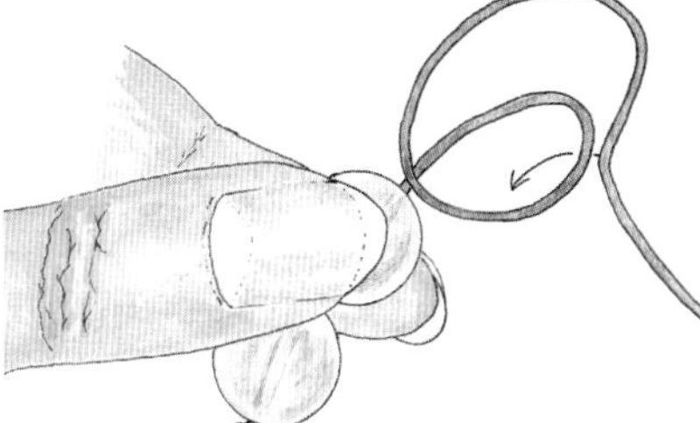
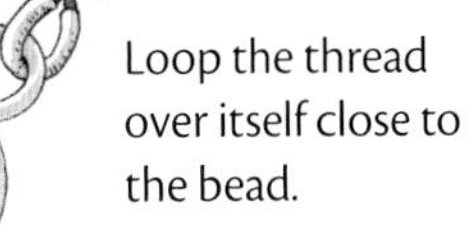
B

Loop the thread over itself close to the bead.

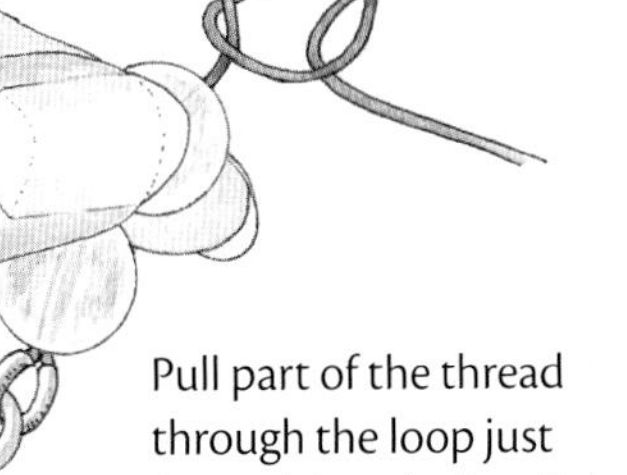
C

Pull part of the thread through the loop just formed, but don't pull the end of the thread through.

Pick up the threads with forefingers and thumbs in the positions indicated by the arrows and slowly pull apart; this has the effect of pulling the knot down towards the bead.

D

When you are satisfied that the knot is tight up against the bead, pass the loose end of thread through the loop.

E

Gently pull the thread through the loop, but be careful to do this slowly or the thread will twist.

F

4 Thread on one more quartz bead followed by the smaller bead sequence as shown in the photograph and another quartz bead (no knots between any of these beads). Continue threading, knotting only between the sequence of three quartz beads.

5 Do not knot between the last two beads to be threaded, but instead thread on the remaining length of gimp and the other part of the clasp before threading back through the last bead, tying an overhand knot and sealing with superglue, as in Step 2.

Emerald

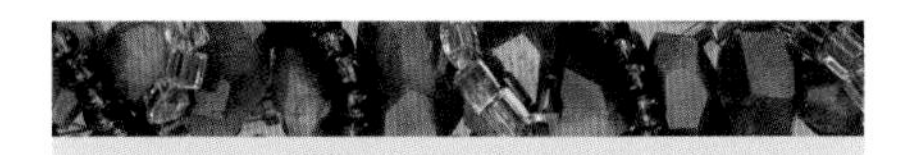

APPEARANCE AND COLOUR
Best quality clear and bright, lesser quality opaque or with inclusions; green

AVAILABILITY IN BEAD FORM
Rare and usually not high quality

COUNTRIES OF ORIGIN
Australia, Austria, Brazil, Columbia, India, Tanzania, USA, Zimbabwe

Emerald is one of a group of precious stones known as beryl, of which aquamarine is a pale version. The brilliant green of emerald is conferred by the presence of chromium during its formation, and the brighter and clearer the colour, the higher its value – the best stones can command an even higher price than diamonds. However, unlike diamonds it is possible to purchase emerald in bead form.

Emerald is one of our most prized stones, so it is not surprising that it has many reputed magical powers, among which are an ability to enhance memory, attract love, enable eloquent speech, promote business dealings and alleviate the effects of misfortune and emotional problems. It is also said to be beneficial for those suffering from ill health, and wearing or holding the stone is believed to aid recovery from sinus, heart, muscular, liver and infective problems.

BUYER'S GUIDE

Emerald is expensive in bead form, but you can use glass substitutes to good effect.

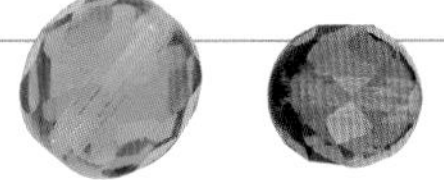

The Real Deal

Time to make 40 minutes • **Ease of making** 2 • **Length** 44cm (17½in)

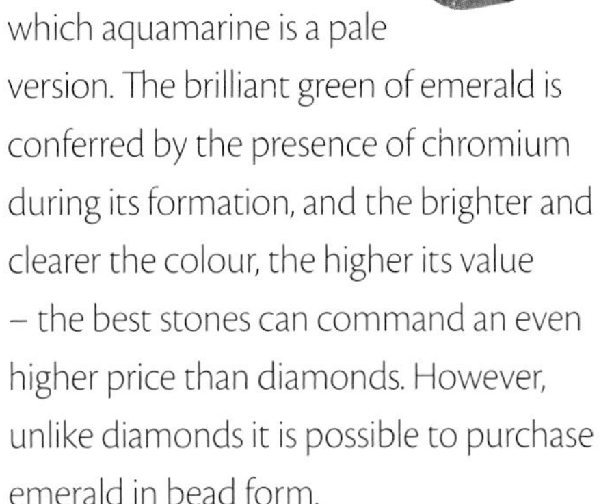

This necklace was made from a graduated string of relatively poor-quality yet expensive emeralds, but they have a look that says 'this is the real thing' enhanced by a 9-carat gold clasp. Normally, I prefer to knot between valuable beads, but because of the tiny holes, this was impossible and I had to use a bead reamer several times. So, for a strong but flexible threading medium, I used fine nylon-coated wire, secured to the clasp with 'gold' gimp and goldfill crimp beads (see page 15).

Let's Pretend

Time to make pendant 1½ hours; earrings 15 minutes • **Ease of making** pendant 4; earrings 3 • **Length** pendant 44cm (17½in); earrings 6cm (2½in)

When making Let's Pretend, I intended to make a simple necklace and earrings set using less expensive beads as a substitute for emerald and so the main part of the necklace is made from erinite-coloured Swarovski crystal. Then, at a 'rocks and gems' show, I came across a gorgeous piece of moldovite. It proved irresistible and fits so well with emerald that it formed the central pendant of the necklace.

Moldovite has a fascinating history. It was formed nearly 15 million years ago when a meteorite fell to earth, causing enormous heat that vaporized both itself and the surrounding rock. The resulting vapour rose to the ionosphere, from where, after cooling, it fell back to earth to the only place in the world where it can be found – Moldova. The combination of elements from both earth and space are said to give moldovite especially powerful energies for healing and good fortune.

The earrings, shown opposite, are simple to make, with the beads threaded on 'gold' nylon-coated wire – follow the instructions for Using Nylon-coated Wire with Crimp Beads, pages 14 and 17. The main body of the pendant is also simple to make – follow the instructions for Using Nylon-coated Wire with Gimp and Crimp Beads, page 15.

Although rare, and becoming more so, moldovite is still fairly easy to obtain, but it is expensive. So if you want a piece, seek it out before the source has yielded up all its treasures!

INGREDIENTS

- 1 piece of moldovite, teardrop if possible, about 14 x 13mm
- 6 Swarovski bicone beads, 6mm
- 6 Swarovski bicone beads, 5mm
- 28 Swarovski bicone beads, 4mm
- 6 Swarovski bicone beads, 5mm
- 6 gold-plated fancy rondel beads, 3mm
- 28 goldfill beads, 2mm
- 1 gold-plated toggle clasp
- 2 goldfill crimp beads
- 2 x 8mm (⅜in) lengths of 'gold' gimp
- 40cm (16in) length of fine green jewellery wire
- 53cm (21in) length of nylon-coated wire

1 Fold a 12cm (5in) length of the jewellery wire over four times at one end (diagram A). Twist these four lengths together until they form a 'rope', leaving a small loop at the end (diagram B).

2 Use the 'rope' to fold over the top of your pendant, to form the loop for threading. With the remaining single thickness, bind the wire tightly to the pendant, using the roughness of the stone to give grip and the loop at the end of the rope to give anchorage. Continue until you are happy with the result and the pendant is securely held. Tuck the end of the wire out of sight and trim the spare wire. Use your pliers to press the cut end in so that it will not scratch you when wearing your necklace.

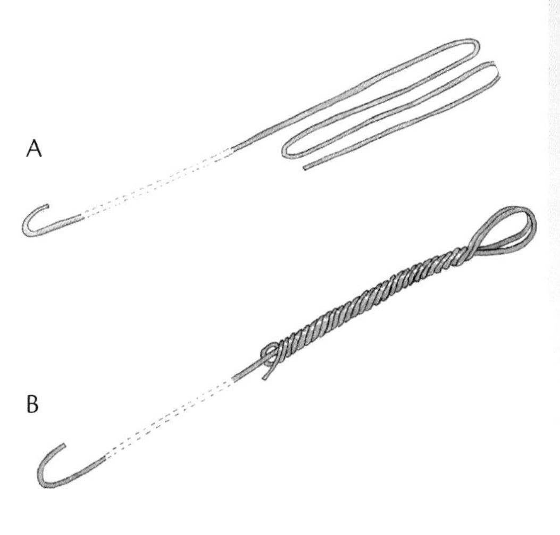

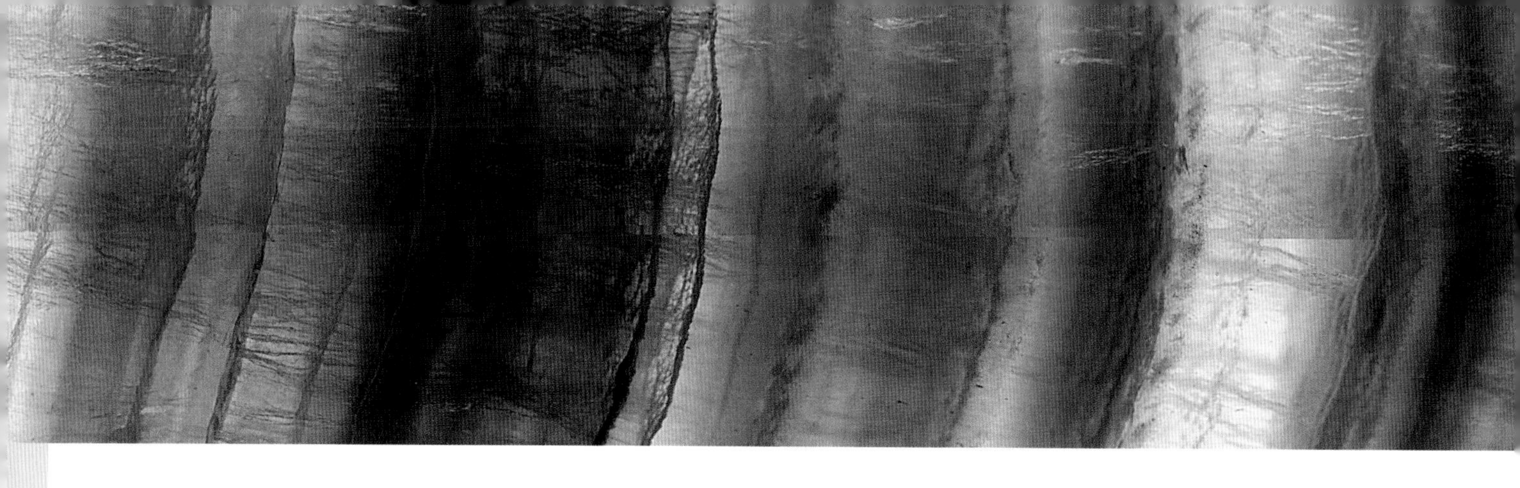

Fluorite

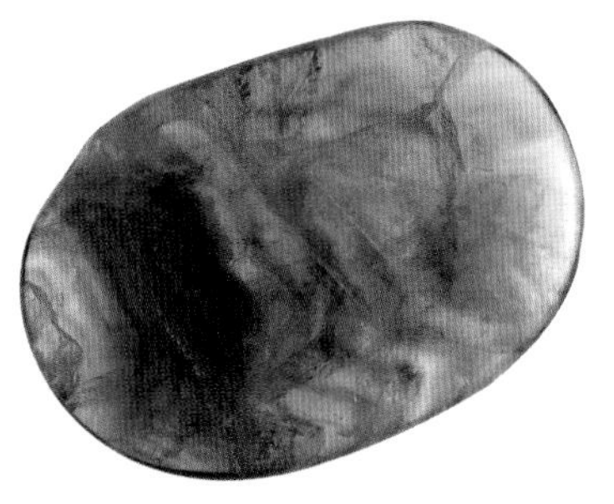

Fluorite occurs in octahedral or cubic crystals, sometimes in a single colour, but more often in bands of differing hues, the latter variety called rainbow fluorite. The main 'magical power' of fluorite is to bring order to chaos, an attribute that is said also to work in the mind, where it improves concentration and analytical ability. As a result, fluorite has become known as the stone of responsibility. Wearing fluorite is thought to bring emotional stability by lifting depression and despair, and dispelling anger. It is reputed to be an aid to good health and physical perfection.

Many fluorite stones are fluorescent, that is, when exposed to ultraviolet light they glow, which may be the origin of the stone's name. This characteristic often turns the stone into a very different colour; green fluorite seen in ultraviolet light may appear dark purple and mauve may appear green, for example. When heated to a temperature above 100°C (212°F), some fluorite stones will also give off a visible light.

APPEARANCE AND COLOUR
Clear or translucent in bands of colour; blue, green, yellow, brown and purple

AVAILABILITY IN BEAD FORM
Common

COUNTRIES OF ORIGIN
Australia, Brazil, Canada, China, Germany, Italy, Mexico, Norway, Peru

BUYER'S GUIDE

For a stone with such a dramatic appearance, rainbow fluorite is very inexpensive. It therefore makes a good choice if you are on a budget yet looking for something spectacular.

Floral Drops

Time to make 1 hour • **Ease of making** 4 • **Length** 53cm (21in), plus 15cm (6in) drop

It is hard to find prettier mineral material than fluorite, and this necklace displays all the beauty of the stone and its gorgeous array of colours. Each of the large stones is fluorite, the feature fluorite bead being rectangular and 25 x 17mm, but you can use any large bead. To enhance the effect, I have added a few lustre-coated rocailles and some tiny 'silver' bead caps.

The necklace is simple to make, and even an inexperienced beader should be able to complete it in two hours.

Despite its good looks, this necklace is inexpensive to make, costing no more than a necklace made from good-quality glass beads.

INGREDIENTS

- 1 fluorite feature bead
- 28 green baroque fluorite beads, 10–12mm
- 11 mixed-colour fluorite flower beads, 12mm
- 9 mixed-colour fluorite barrel beads, 6 x 4mm
- a few mauve medium AB-coated rocaille beads
- a few clear small AB-coated rocaille beads
- 2 silver-plated bead caps, 8mm
- 32 silver-plated bead caps, 4mm
- 1 silver-plated 2-hole spacer bar
- 1 silver-plated toggle clasp
- 2 x 8mm (⅜in) lengths of 'silver' gimp
- 6 'silver' crimp beads (one hidden inside the feature bead)
- 2 x 50cm (20in) lengths of nylon-coated wire
- 20cm (8in) length of nylon-coated wire

A

1 Using gimp and a crimp bead, attach one end of one of the 50cm (20in) lengths of wire to one part of the clasp (see Using Nylon-coated Wire with Gimp and Crimp Beads, page 15).

2 Using the photograph as a guide, thread on beads in the sequence shown, finishing after threading the first 8mm bead cap.

3 Lay this part of the necklace to one side while you repeat Steps 1–2 with the remaining 50cm (20in) length of wire for the other side of the necklace. When you reach the spacer bar, thread down through the remaining hole and continue as shown in the photograph, so that both wires emerge together from below the first 8mm bead cap.

4 Lay the two strands on a flat surface in front of you and thread a crimp bead over both to sit about 1cm (⅜in) from the 8mm bead cap, then thread one end of the 20cm (8in) length of wire through the crimp bead (diagram A).

5 Push the threaded beads up to the clasp ends to make sure that the feature bead, once threaded, will cover the crimp bead. When you are happy with the position of the crimp bead, squeeze it in place to secure all three wires together (see Using Nylon-coated Wire with Crimp Beads, page 14).

6 Thread on the feature bead, followed by the remaining 8mm bead cap. The previously threaded crimp bead should now be hidden from sight and three wires will be hanging from beneath the feature bead and 8mm bead cap.

7 Using the photograph as a guide, thread the three free lengths of wire with the remaining beads. Ensuring that each is a different length for a graceful effect, apply a crimp bead to the end of each length of wire as before. Be careful not to take up all the slack in the wire, otherwise the beaded tassels will hang stiffly. Finish the necklace by trimming the spare wire.

Cascade

Time to make 2 hours • **Ease of making** 5 • **Length** 64cm (25in)

Featuring many of the different colours of fluorite, this stunning necklace costs surprisingly little and is also easy to make. To help reduce the cost and also to introduce variety of size and texture, I have combined the fluorite beads with small faceted Czech glass beads and two different types of mauve/purple AB-coated rocailles.

The most expensive components of the necklace are the two heavyweight sterling silver cones, but I feel the extra cost is worthwhile, as they add a special look of quality. Although there are a large number of beads to be threaded, this necklace can be tackled by anyone, even those new to beading.

The rainbow colours of fluorite are so beautiful that the crystals were known to miners as 'ore flowers'. However, this is a fragile beauty, as the stone is soft, so to protect your finished fluorite jewellery, treat it with care and avoid contact with sharp objects.

1 Check that the five lengths of wire will pass through each of the large fluorite beads and, if necessary, enlarge the holes with a bead reamer (see page 13).

2 Arrange the large beads on a tray so that their appearance is pleasing, i.e. with the smaller beads towards the ends of the necklace and the colours suitably distributed.

3 Thread the five lengths of wire together through a crimp bead. Use a pair of general-purpose pliers to squeeze the crimp bead in place near the end of the wire. After checking that this is securely in place, trim any spare wire as close as possible to the crimp bead.

INGREDIENTS

- 8 mixed-colour baroque fluorite beads, 18–20mm
- 2 fluorite flower beads, 12mm
- 40cm (16in) string of rainbow fluorite beads, 6mm
- 40cm (16in) string of rainbow fluorite barrel beads, 6 x 4mm
- 84 pale mauve AB-coated faceted Czech glass beads, 4mm
- 2 small packets of mauve/purple AB-coated rocaille beads: 1 silver-lined, 1 transparent
- 2 sterling silver necklace cones, 20mm
- 2 silver-plated bead caps, 12mm
- 2 silver-plated cone-shaped bead caps, 9mm
- 1 silver-plated toggle clasp
- 2 crimp beads (hidden)
- 2 'silver' clamshell calottes
- 5 x 75cm (30in) lengths of nylon-coated wire

The large beads used for this necklace were taken from a ready-made stretchy bracelet to save the waste beads that would arise from purchasing a 40cm (16in) string of beads.

The British variety of fluorite is found in Derbyshire, where it is known as blue John.

4 Thread the five wires through the hole in a clamshell calotte and pull them through so that the crimp bead sits inside the hollow of the calotte (diagram A). Use the pliers to close the calotte over the wire end and crimp bead.

5 Thread all five wires through a cone-shaped bead cap, then, using the photograph as a guide, thread each of the wires with beads in the sequences shown. Pass all five wires through one of the necklace cones, a flower bead, a 12mm bead cap and the large fluorite beads, followed by the remaining 12mm bead cap, flower bead and necklace cone.

6 Thread the five wires with beads to match the finished side of the necklace, then thread all five wires through the remaining clamshell calotte and crimp bead.

7 Adjust the threaded wires so that all the lengths are equal and there is enough play for the necklace to hang correctly without distortion, but also ensuring that there is little bare wire visible, then close the calotte over the wire end and crimp bead with pliers, as before.

8 Attach the clasp to the loops of the two calottes (see page 15).

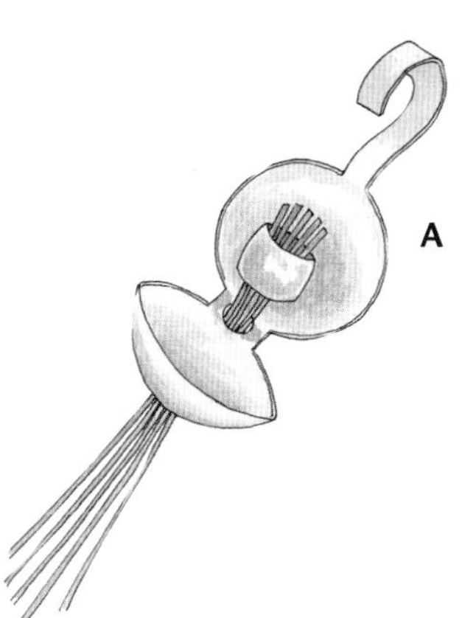

The polishing of all stones brings out their real beauty, but even the unpolished stones can look impressive, as seen here in this piece of fluorite that has been polished on one side only, leaving the other just as nature formed it.

Rainbow Drops

Time to make 40 minutes • **Ease of making** 3 • **Length** 8cm (3in)

Here, another style of fluorite bead lends itself perfectly to an elegant pair of drop earrings. Exhibiting even more of the range of fluorite colours available, these flat disc beads are unusual yet, as with most fluorite, inexpensive. The earrings are simple to make and are threaded on attractive 'gold' nylon-coated wire.

INGREDIENTS

- ✧ 8 mixed-colour fluorite disc beads
- ✧ 8 goldfill oval beads, 5 x 3mm
- ✧ 16 gold-plated plain washer beads
- ✧ 2 green anodized niobium jump rings
- ✧ 10 goldfill crimp beads
- ✧ 1 pair of goldfill ear-hooks
- ✧ 4 x 15cm (6in) lengths of 'gold' nylon-coated wire

1 Thread two of the lengths of wire through one of the crimp beads so that they form small, evenly matched loops (diagram A) and the ends hang at different lengths. Use pliers (crimp pliers if possible) to secure the crimp bead in place.

2 Using the photograph as a guide, thread the beads onto each wire. When you are happy with the length of each thread, apply a crimp bead to secure the beads in place. Check that each crimp bead is securely in place, then trim the spare wire as close to the crimp beads as possible.

3 Open up a jump ring sideways and thread on the loop of an ear-hook, then thread on the loops of the earring drop before closing the ring (see Using Thong or Cord with Box Calottes and Jump Rings, page 16).

4 Make up the other earring in the same way, making sure that the lengths of wire match those of the first earring.

Garnet

This well-loved and familiar stone has been used in jewellery for thousands of years, and still today the red form of the stone is very popular in both rings and pendants. Perhaps because most gemstone garnets are blood red, the stone has come to signify health and strength, and for those requiring endurance, it is reputed to given them the capacity to carry on performing arduous tasks without being overcome by tiredness.

Wearing or carrying garnet is said to protect from danger by creating a protective shield that turns evil away from the wearer. It is also a stone for love and is believed to enhance passion as well as confidence. In terms of health, garnet is worn to aid the heart, lungs and the metabolism.

APPEARANCE AND COLOUR
Transparent, translucent or opaque; rich red, pink, green, orange, yellow, brown or black

AVAILABILITY IN BEAD FORM
Small beads easily available; larger beads less common

COUNTRIES OF ORIGIN
Worldwide

BUYER'S GUIDE

For such a beautiful stone, most garnet is surprisingly inexpensive.

Glamour

Time to make 30 minutes • **Ease of making** 2 • **Length** 22cm (8¾in)

This gorgeous chunky bracelet is made from unusually large garnet beads taken from a 40cm (16in) string. The method of making it is simple – just follow the instructions for Using Nylon-coated Wire with Gimp and Crimp Beads, page 15. I have used red gimp, but you could use 'gold' and still achieve a look of quality. Because the beads are heavy and have a large hole, I have used two lengths of nylon-coated wire for extra strength. No ingredient list is given, as it is easy to see from the photograph what items are required.

Romance

Time to make necklace 2 hours; earrings 20 minutes • **Ease of making** necklace 4; earrings 3 • **Length** necklace 61cm (24in); earrings 7cm (2¾in)

This necklace and earrings set shows off the rich colour of garnet and combines three different styles of bead. The smallest ones are left threaded on their original thread because they were already well strung and their holes are minuscule, which would make re-threading 750 of them a daunting task!

The earrings are simple to make using leftover ingredients from the necklace – use the photograph as a guide to the design and threading, and follow the instructions for Using Headpins, page 16.

INGREDIENTS

- ✧ 1 baroque faceted garnet bead, 18–20mm
- ✧ 40cm (16in) string of baroque oval garnet beads, 8 x 6mm
- ✧ 4 x 40cm (16in) strings of garnet beads, 2mm
- ✧ 1 gold-plated bead cap, 8mm
- ✧ 2 gold-plated bead caps, 7mm
- ✧ 3 gold-plated bead caps, 3mm
- ✧ 1 gold-plated bail
- ✧ 1 gold-plated toggle clasp
- ✧ 1 gold-plated headpin
- ✧ 4 goldfill crimp beads
- ✧ 2 gold-plated clamshell calottes
- ✧ 4 x 8mm (⅜in) lengths of red (or 'gold') gimp
- ✧ 2 x 18cm (7in) lengths of fine nylon-coated wire
- ✧ bottle of liquid superglue

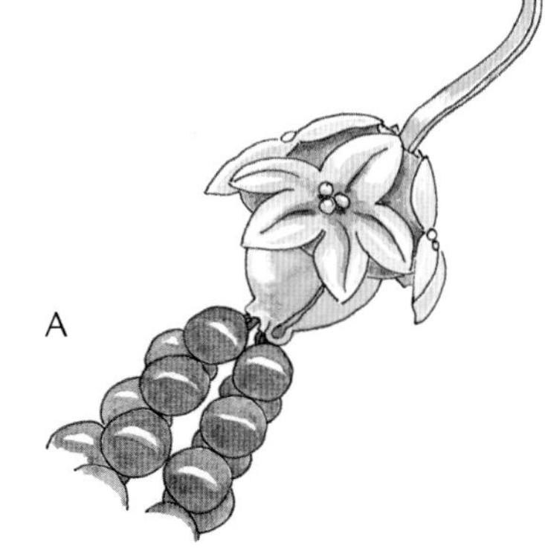

A

1 Using the photograph as a guide to the threading and the instructions for Using Headpins, page 16, make up the large garnet bead pendant on the gold-plated bail.

2 Undo the knots of the 2mm bead lengths and remove an 8cm (3in) length of beads from each string. Make sure that the remaining lengths are equal, then thread one end of each string together through the hole of one clamshell calotte. Tie a single overhand knot in all the thread ends together so that it sits inside the calotte 'shell', trim the spare threads and close the calotte (see Using Beading Thread with Clamshell Calottes, page 15).

3 Slide the bail over the strands of beads until it is in the centre. This could be a tight fit, so take care not to damage any beads.

4 Open the loop of the calotte and slide a 7mm bead cap over the open loop, then close the loop (diagram A). Repeat Steps 2–4 with the other ends of the strings.

5 Using the nylon-coated wire, gimp and crimp beads, make up two 13in (5in) strands of baroque oval garnet beads as shown (see Using Nylon-coated Wire with Gimp and Crimp Beads, page 15). For each strand, attach one end to the clasp and the other to the calotte loop of the central beaded section.

Hematite

Ask hematite a question! In a darkened room, hold a piece of hematite so that the light of a red candle is reflected on its surface. Mentally voice your query and the answer may be revealed to you!

Hematite is rich in iron ore and as such is a valuable commodity in industry. But as you can see, it is also a popular jewellery stone that is available in a vast range of bead sizes and shapes.

In terms of psychological well-being, the stone is reputed to enhance courage, relieve stress, balance energy and emotions and encourage positive thinking, harmony and love. It is also believed to help develop mathematical skills, memory and original, creative ideas.

As might be expected from a stone rich in iron, hematite is considered to be beneficial to the circulatory system. It is also said to help regenerate tissue, aid the kidneys, dispel insomnia and generally to draw sickness from the body.

APPEARANCE AND COLOUR
Opaque rusty red or dull black in rough state; metallic shiny black when polished

AVAILABILITY IN BEAD FORM
Common, especially in reconstituted form known as hematine

COUNTRIES OF ORIGIN
Australia, Brazil, Canada, Italy, Sweden, Switzerland, UK, USA

Hema Hatpin

Time to make 5 minutes • **Ease of making** 1 • **Length** 12.5cm (5in)

This elegant item is easily made by simply threading the beads in the sequence shown in the photograph onto a 12.5cm (5in) hatpin. Before threading the last bead and bead cap, put a little superglue onto the hatpin where these two items will 'sit' and then slide the beads up tight to the others to hold them firmly in place. Never use superglue for this purpose with valuable beads or if there is any chance that you will later wish to re-use the beads, as the glue will ruin the bead for threading.

BUYER'S GUIDE

Real hematite is becoming less common in bead form, but hematine is a reconstituted substitute (seen here) that is readily available in many sizes and shapes.

Magnetism

Time to make 40 minutes • **Ease of making** 1 • **Length** 86cm (34in)

INGREDIENTS

- 45 magnetic cube beads, 5mm
- 216 deep blue (or any other colour) large rocaille beads
- 2 goldfill crimp beads
- 92cm (36in) length of nylon-coated wire

Because hematite is an iron-based ore, it can be magnetized, so here is a fun item made from gold-coloured hematine and large rocailles, which can be worn in various styles of necklace or as a bracelet and without a clasp, since the beads stick to each other. The beads are merely threaded onto nylon-coated wire and the ends secured with crimp beads (see page 14).

Black Ice

Time to make 1 hour • **Ease of making** 3 • **Length** 40cm (16in), plus 9cm (3½in) drops

This necklace has a look of quality despite a low cost, and I am sure it will have a universal appeal due to its fluidity of movement and elegant appearance. The teardrop and bicone beads are reconstituted hematite, which are, almost without exception, flawless and identical, so there is no need to seek out matching beads.

INGREDIENTS

- 3 hematine teardrop beads, 15 x 8mm
- 8 hematine bicone beads 5 x 4mm
- 20 hematine-coloured twisted bugle beads, 10mm
- 20 'gold' matt-finish large rocaille beads
- 50 gold-plated flat rondel beads, 3mm
- 4 gold-plated heart links
- 1 gold-plated toggle clasp
- 14 goldfill crimp beads
- 4 gold-plated headpins
- 2 gold-plated box calottes
- 2 gold-plated jump rings
- 61cm (24in) length of black rat-tail, 2mm
- 7 x 12cm (4¾in) lengths of nylon-coated wire

1 Using the lengths of nylon-coated wire and the crimp beads, make up the drops as shown in the photograph (see Using Nylon-coated Wire with Crimp Beads, pages 14 and 17), making sure that the top loops are large enough for threading onto the rat-tail. After securing the crimp beads, trim any spare wire.

2 Using the headpins, attach the remaining bicone beads to the heart links.

3 Thread the central drop onto the length of rat-tail and secure it in the centre by tying an overhand knot either side of the loop. Thread on the other drops one by one, tying an overhand knot in the rat-tail after each.

4 Check and if necessary trim the length of the rat-tail. Apply a box calotte to either end (see Using Thong or Cord with Box Calottes and Jump Rings, page 16), then use the jump rings to attach the clasp.

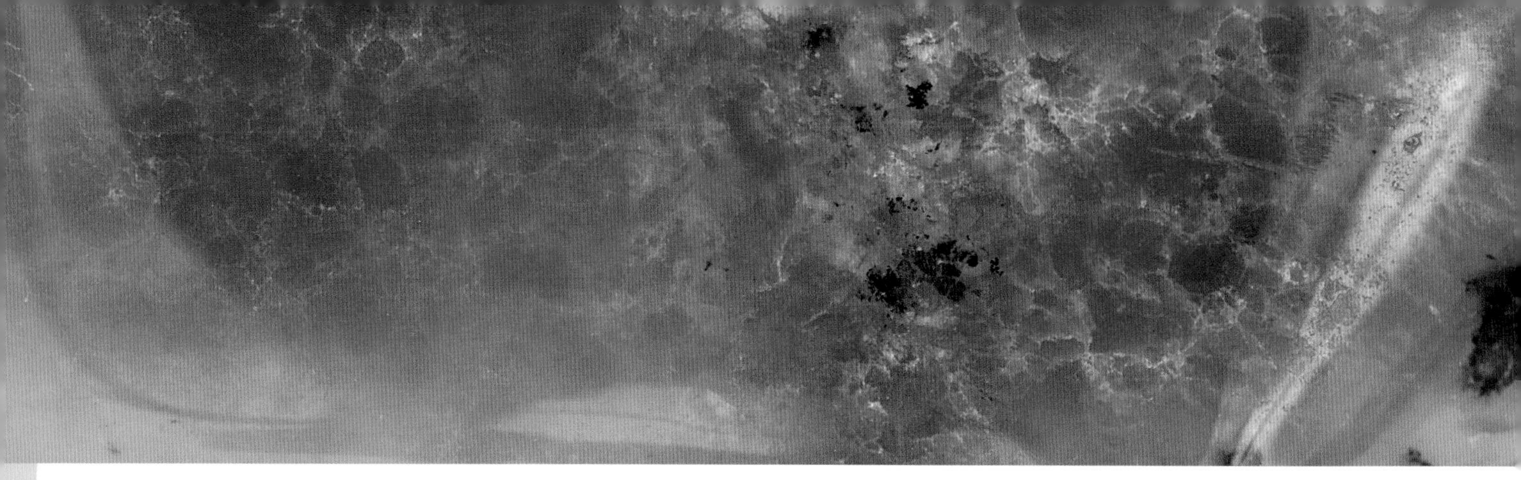

Jade

The best jade is considered to be a gemstone and is a beautiful bright green

We all think of jade as green, and while it is true that the most prized jade is bright green, there are also a great many variations. These are created, in part, by the fact that under the umbrella term 'jade' there are several different stone types. Traditionally, these are nephrite and jadeite, but in more recent years soo chow jade (alternatively called Chinese new jade or bowenite) and chrysoprase or Australian jade have fallen under the same collective name.

In China, the gift of jade is a gift of love, which is considered especially lucky if the stone is carved into the shape of a butterfly. This belief arose from an ancient tale of a young lad who, in heedless pursuit of a colourful butterfly, stumbled into the garden of a mandarin. Instead of punishing the intruder, the wealthy man chose to give him his beautiful daughter in marriage. Consequently, even now, this gift from man to woman is believed to confer happy and successful love.

Jade has long been utilized for healing, particularly in relation to treating problems of the kidneys, spleen and heart. It is also believed to be especially beneficial in attracting wealth and good luck in business dealings.

Gardeners are considered to gain advantage from the powers of jade, and either wearing a piece or burying it in the garden is said to ensure the healthy growth of plants. Jade is also believed to be lucky for travellers, who are reputed to be protected from danger when wearing the stone.

APPEARANCE AND COLOUR
Translucent or opaque; green, blue/green, blue, pale mauve, yellow, red/orange, brown, cream or white

AVAILABILITY IN BEAD FORM
Most stone types are readily available

COUNTRIES OF ORIGIN
Canada, China, Italy, Mexico, Middle East, Myanmar, New Zealand, Russia, USA

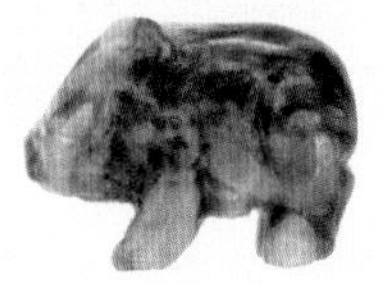

BUYER'S GUIDE

The price of jade varies greatly with the quality and type of the stone. New jade may be purchased at little cost, while the best-quality bright emerald green jadeite is very expensive.

Chinese Knot

Time to make 1½ hours • **Ease of making** 4 • **Length** 54cm (21in), plus 14cm (5½in) drop

The two traditional jades, nephrite and jadeite, can be difficult to distinguish from one another, and so it is with the beads and pendant in this necklace! I believe they are nephrite, but they were simply sold to me as antiqued jade. However, whatever their exact nature, they are jade and have a beautifully subtle colouring and etched pattern that is perfect for this necklace.

Brown jade is a grounding stone that enhances oneness with the earth and environment. It could therefore be a suitable gift to someone who is moving to another country, area or house.

INGREDIENTS

- 1 brown jade flat pendant with multiple holes, 40mm
- 40cm (16in) string of brown jade, 10mm
- 10 sterling silver barrel beads, 2.5 x 6mm
- 58 silver-plated faceted bicone beads, 3mm
- packet of clear brown small rocaille beads
- 1 silver-plated toggle clasp
- 15 sterling silver crimp beads (6 are hidden from sight)
- 2 silver-plated clamshell calottes
- 61cm (24in) length of nylon-coated wire
- 20cm (8in) length of nylon-coated wire
- 5 x 8cm (3in) lengths of nylon-coated wire

Nephrite jade is an extremely tough material with a higher elastic strength than steel. When held in the hand it has a waxy feel and makes a tactile pocket stone – like the polished worry-stone seen here.

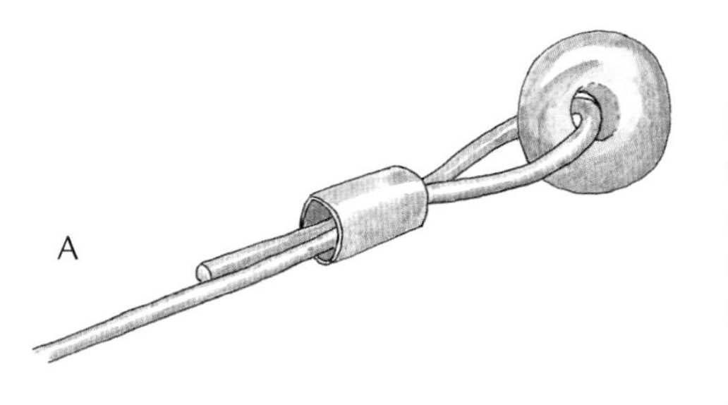

In New Zealand, Maoris handed heirloom pieces from father to son, in the belief that the stone conferred good fortune and had powers over the weather, while in Mexico the Mayans believed that jade was a bringer of harmony.

1 Start by making up the pendant. Thread onto the end of one of the 8cm (3in) lengths of nylon-coated wire a crimp bead and a rocaille bead, thread back up through the crimp bead and squeeze closed with your pliers to hold the rocaille tightly in place at the end of the wire (diagram A).

2 Thread on one of the 10mm jade beads so that the crimp bead is hidden beneath the bead and only the small rocaille bead is seen.

3 Thread on the remaining beads as shown in the photograph, then make a loop and attach the drop to the appropriate hole in the pendant (see Using Nylon-coated Wire with Crimp Beads, pages 14 and 17). Complete the remaining drops in the same way.

4 Thread the 20cm (8in) length of nylon-coated wire through the top hole of the pendant and then thread on a crimp bead. Making sure that the two lengths of wire are even, squeeze the crimp bead to secure in place at a distance from the pendant where it will be covered by a 10mm jade bead.

5 Thread onto both ends of the wire together one 10mm jade bead and one faceted bicone bead. Thread onto each wire separately the rocaille and silver barrel bead sequences as shown in the photograph. Use another crimp bead to secure a small loop in the end of each length of wire, as in Step 3, then trim the wire.

6 Using a crimp bead and one of the clamshell calottes, attach the remaining length of nylon-coated wire to one part of the clasp (see Using Nylon-coated Wire with Crimp Beads and Clamshell Calottes, page 15).

7 Thread on the bead sequence as shown in the photograph, and when you have threaded the last bead before the central one, thread through one of the loops of the pendant. Continue threading as shown, then in the same position as before, thread through the remaining loop of the pendant so that it is suspended evenly at either side of the centre of the necklace.

8 Continue threading as shown, then attach the other part of the clasp, as in Step 6.

Triple Drop

Time to make 30 minutes • **Ease of making** 3 • **Length** 8cm (3¼in)

So what do you do if you have just a few beads left over and you want to make a jade jewellery item? Well, here is the answer. These elegant, drop-style earrings are made using just two jade beads each. The large, 9mm beads are soo chow jade – strictly speaking, not real jade. However, the smaller, 4mm beads are the variety of real jade known as nephrite.

I have chosen to use anodized niobium ear-hooks in a colour to match the jade, which can be made up following Step 6 on page 16. The drops are suspended on headpins and linked to the large silver-plated loop links by jump rings (see pages 16–17 for techniques).

INGREDIENTS

- 2 soo chow jade beads, 9mm
- 2 nephrite jade beads, 4mm
- 6 peacock-coloured twisted bugles, 10mm
- 4 silver-plated fancy square beads, 6mm
- 4 sterling silver oval beads, 3 x 5mm
- 6 sterling silver beads, 2mm
- 6 small green rocaille beads
- 2 silver-plated bead caps, 5mm
- 6 silver-plated bead caps, 3mm
- 2 silver-plated loop links
- 6 silver-plated headpins
- 8 silver-plated jump rings
- 1 pair of green anodized niobium straight-leg ear-hooks

Aussie Gem

Time to make 1 hour • **Ease of making** 4 • **Length** 46cm (18in), plus 5cm (2in) drop

Chrysoprase (Australian jade) in its best form is a valuable gemstone. The polished chunk seen opposite and the pendant in the necklace are chrysoprase, but not of the finest quality and therefore inexpensive. In reality, it is not a jade and, as a separate stone, has it own attributes, among which are a reputation for enhancing creativity, light-heartedness and eloquence, while bringing calmness, peaceful sleep and fertility.

In this necklace I have combined chrysoprase with soo chow jade, as the two stone types complement each other well. This pale, milky green Chinese stone is inexpensive to purchase and easy to obtain.

The earrings are made using some of the spare beads from the necklace, together with two more oval new jade beads. Use the photograph as a guide to threading and follow the instructions for Using Headpins and Multiple Headpins, pages 16–17.

INGREDIENTS

- 1 piece of polished chrysoprase, 40 x 25mm
- 40cm (16in) string of cushion-shaped soo chow beads, 7 x 4mm
- 16 silver-plated fancy rondel beads, 8mm
- 2 silver-plated fancy rondel beads, 6mm
- a few pearlized pale green small rocaille beads
- 1 silver-plated toggle clasp
- 2 silver-plated clamshell calottes
- 2 'silver' crimp beads
- 80cm (32in) length of silver-plated fine jewellery wire
- 56cm (22in) length of nylon-coated wire

Jade is considered to be one of the birthstones for Taurus and therefore especially lucky for anyone born under the sign of the bull.

A

1 Bend the length of fine jewellery wire into two equal lengths, then twist these together to make a 40cm (16in) length of 'rope' with a small loop at one end (diagram A).

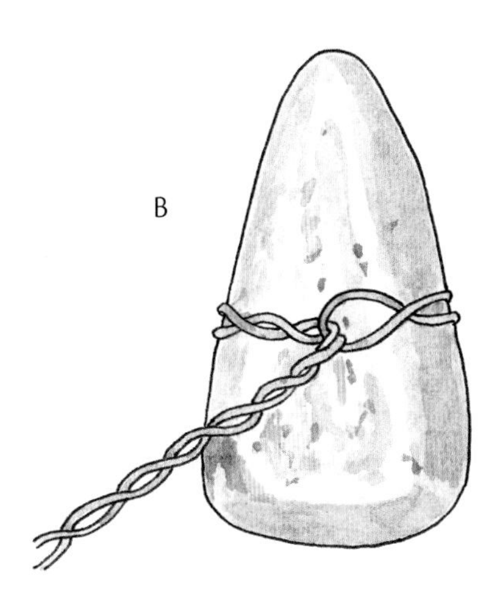

2 Begin winding the rope around the piece of polished chrysoprase, using the small loop to anchor the first circuit of the stone (diagram B). Continue winding the wire around the stone, anchoring it by looping the wire over and around itself as you go. Be sure to keep the wire taut at all times. Continue until you are satisfied with the appearance of the pendant and the stone is held securely (you may need several attempts), then bring the wire to the top of the pendant, anchoring it as you go.

3 At the top of the pendant, bend the wire over again so that there are now four thicknesses together and twist it once more. Form a loop in the wire (for attachment to the necklace), then wind the wire tightly around the base of the loop to secure it. Trim the spare wire and tuck the cut ends into the wound wire to hide from view.

4 Using a crimp bead and one of the clamshell calottes, attach the remaining length of nylon-coated wire to one part of the clasp (see Using Nylon-coated Wire with Crimp Beads and Clamshell Calottes, page 15). Thread on the beads in the sequence shown in the photograph, threading on the pendant in the centre, then attach the other part of the clasp, as before.

Waves

Time to make 1 hour • **Ease of making** 4 • **Length** 21.5cm (8½in)

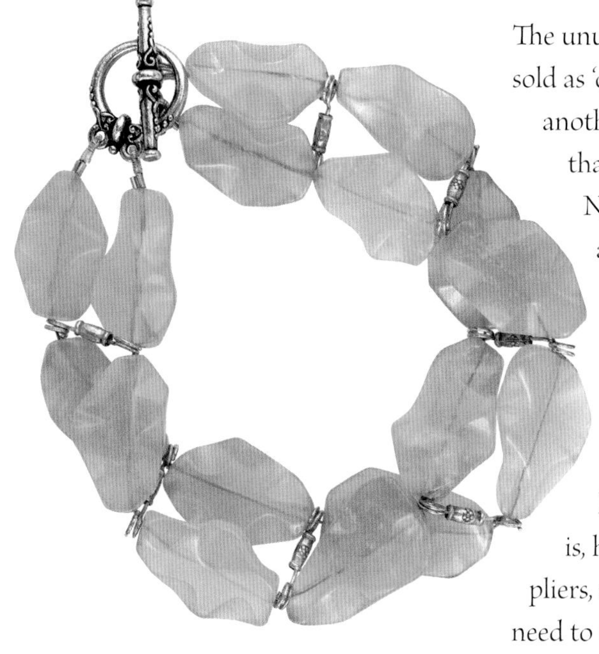

The unusual wavy beads in this bracelet were sold as 'oil jade,' but I believe this to be yet another name for soo chow jade and also that the beads may be colour-enhanced. Nevertheless, they are interesting and attractive, and lend themselves well to this style of bracelet.

It is easy to find ready-made connectors for bracelets such as this, but here I have made my own so that they are exactly the correct length for the beads. To make them, it is, however, essential to use round-nosed pliers, so if you don't own a pair, you will need to use ready-made connectors instead.

INGREDIENTS

- 40cm (16in) string of wavy-edged soo chow jade beads, about 20 x 15mm
- 7 sterling silver barrel beads, 2.5 x 6mm
- 1 silver-plated clasp for 2 threads
- 7 silver-plated headpins, 5cm (2in)
- 4 sterling silver crimp beads
- 4 x 8mm (⅜in) lengths of 'silver' gimp
- 2 x 28cm (11in) lengths of nylon-coated wire

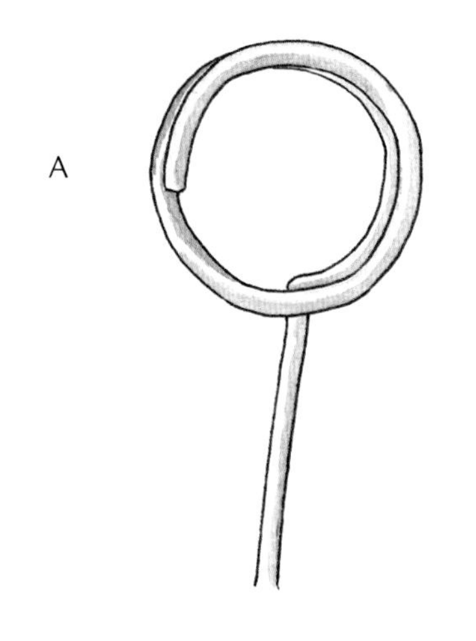

1 Cut off the head of one of the headpins with cutting pliers, then gently grasp the tip of one end of the headpin with your round-nosed pliers, bend the wire around one jaw of the pliers, then release them slightly to allow the wire loop that you are creating to slide further around the jaw. Grasp the wire again and continue forming a round loop until the wire is almost double (diagram A).

2 Thread one of the sterling silver barrel beads onto the wire loop, then form another double loop at the other end of the headpin, as in Step 1. Make up six more connectors in the same way.

3 Using two lengths of the gimp and two crimp beads, attach one end of both lengths of nylon-coated wire to one part of the clasp (see Using Nylon-coated Wire with Gimp and Crimp Beads, page 15). Thread each wire with the bead sequence and connectors as shown in the photograph.

4 Finish by attaching the threaded wires to the other part of the clasp, as in Step 3.

Lucky Gem

Time to make 10 minutes • **Ease of making** 2 • **Length** 40cm (16in)

The pendant bead used for this simple choker is carved from jadeite stone, a material that is attributed with its own powers in addition to those already mentioned for jade in general. These include enhancing understanding and unity between members of groups and families, as well as aiding intelligence, skilled work and insight.

This necklace is very easy to make. It simply involves attaching the pendant to the bail with a triangular jump ring (diagram A) and using the same method to attach the silver-plated cushion-shaped beads to the silver wire. These items are then just threaded onto the ready-made sterling silver cable to complete the choker.

A

INGREDIENTS

- 1 jadeite pendant, 40 x 25cm
- 2 silver-plated fancy cushion-shaped beads
- 1 silver-plated bail
- 3 silver-plated triangular jump rings
- 40cm (16in) length of ready-made sterling silver cable

For thousands of years, the Chinese have believed in the lucky powers of jade and even the poorest would carry a piece with them, while even in modern times a string of jade beads is worn to denote a person of high standing.

If jade is carved into the shape of a three-legged frog or toad, it is traditionally believed by the Chinese to confer especially good fortune. Legend has it that, if on a moonlit night such a frog should appear on your doorstep, monetary wealth will come your way!

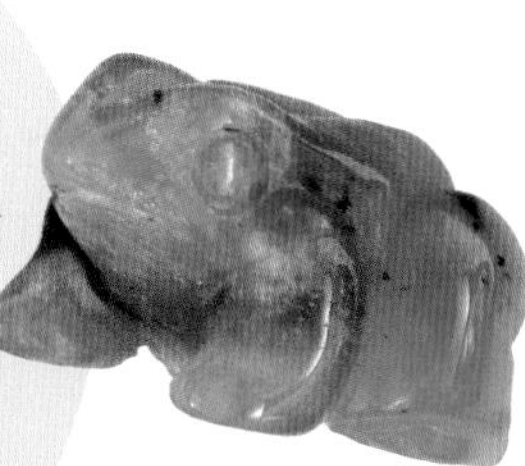

Jasper

Jasper is one of the birthstones for Pisces and would make a perfect birthday gift for anyone with a birthday under this star sign.

Jasper is formed from a combination of chalcedony, quartz and opal, and comes in varieties known by many different names, such as picture, snakeskin, brecciated, galaxy and rainforest. These names are descriptive of the stone's pattern or colour and, without any knowledge of the stones, you should be able to distinguish the various kinds. For example, in a piece of picture jasper you can imagine a scene such as a distant sandy landscape, while the striated surface of snakeskin jasper recalls the shiny smooth skin of its namesake.

From earliest times, jasper has been used by man for practical purposes, adornment and magical practices. As a stone that fractures to leave a conchoidal form (a smooth, round surface resembling a scallop shell), it became an important material for Stone Age man, who used it for making tools, such as arrowheads. Subsequently, these arrowheads became especially prized as good luck emblems. To the Native Americans, green jasper (such as the rainforest jasper seen below left) was known as the rain-bringer and was used in ceremonies to bring life-giving downpours. Later, early immigrants in North America employed it for water divination, maybe taking heed of the Native American folklore! The ancient Greeks, Romans and Egyptians also believed in the protective and healing powers of jasper, using the stone in carvings and amulets.

In general, jasper is reputed to be protective of both physical and mental health, but also considered especially lucky for mother and child when held in the hand during birth. In addition, each colour also has its own special qualities.

APPEARANCE AND COLOUR
Opaque and patterned in shades of brown, grey, cream, yellow, red, blue and green

AVAILABILITY IN BEAD FORM
Common

COUNTRIES OF ORIGIN
Worldwide

BUYER'S GUIDE

Jasper is one of the least expensive stones and available in a huge variety of both large and small bead types. Because many of the colours are earthy, this is one stone that is ideal for a jewellery gift for a man.

Down to Earth

Time to make 2 hours • **Ease of making** 4 • **Length** 69cm (27in)

Down to Earth is a fabulous necklace that seems to go with everything, and I have already worn it many times. In fact, I'm not sure if I can spare it for photography! The beads used are variegated jasper with a random patterned look that appears almost painted on.

Strings of beads such as these are always hand-made and therefore variable in size, so it is advisable to lay all your beads out on a beading tray before stringing so that you thread them in an order that suits their varied sizes, i.e. with the largest beads at the centre of the necklace.

Because this is a long necklace and easily fits over the head, I have not used a clasp but instead just attached the ends of the cotton cord to an attractive metal link. The necklace is fairly simple to make, but a little time-consuming because of the number of loops that have to be made in nylon-coated wire. All the beads in the string were used except for one, which I reserved to make a bracelet suitable for a man. If you can't find these exact beads, this design could be used with any flat bead.

INGREDIENTS

- 40cm (16in) string of wavy variegated jasper beads, 45 x 25 mm
- 1 silver-plated link
- 22 sterling silver crimp beads
- 2 silver-plated box calottes
- 2 silver-plated jump rings
- 11 x 8cm (3in) lengths of nylon-coated wire
- 2 x 90cm (35in) lengths of 1mm waxed cotton cord, 1 brown, 1 black

1 Using a crimp bead, make a loop in one of the lengths of nylon-coated wire (see Using Nylon-coated Wire with Crimp Beads, page 14), making sure that the loop is large enough to take two thicknesses of the cotton cord.

Red jasper is considered to be a stone with great protective powers and when carved with the images of either lions or archers is believed to prevent and cure fevers or poisoning. As a bringer of good things, red jasper is recommended as a stone for young women to wear, as it is reputed to promote elegance and beauty.

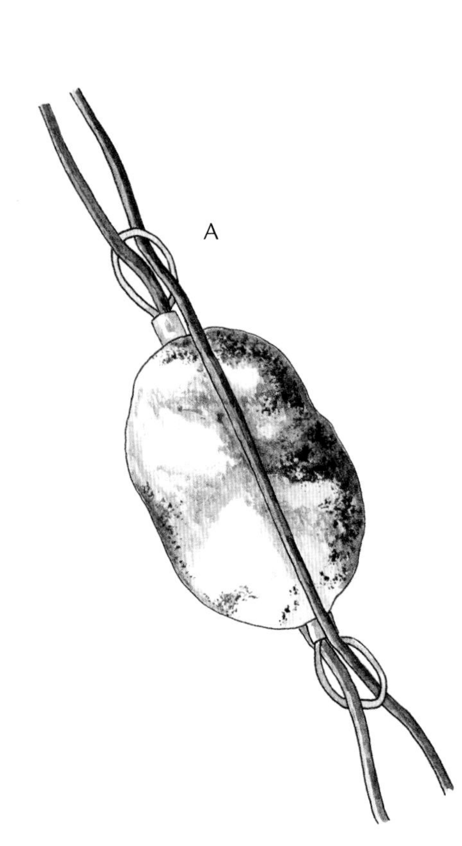

2 Thread one of the jasper beads onto the wire and then make another loop, as in Step 1, keeping it tight to the bead. Trim the spare wire before hiding the cut end inside the hole of the bead.

3 Repeat Steps 1–2 with all the remaining jasper beads, then make sure that they are laid out in your proposed order of threading.

4 Thread one of the lengths of cord through the two wire loops in what will be the central bead so that the cord travels across one side of the bead. Thread the other length of cord through the two wire loops from the opposite direction so that it lies across the other side of the bead (diagram A). Slide the bead to the centre of the two lengths of cord.

5 Repeat Step 4 until all the beads are threaded either side of the central bead, making sure that you keep them in the order of proposed threading if they are of unmatched sizes.

6 Hold the necklace to your neck to decide on the length and then trim any spare cord to equal lengths at either end of the necklace. Secure a box calotte to one end of each pair of cords together, attach jump rings and join the two ends of the necklace together with the link (see Using Thong or Cord with Box Calottes and Jump Rings, page 16).

The earthy colour of brown jasper may account for its main attribute, i.e. it is reputed to bring daydreamers and unrealistic thinkers back to reality – or down to earth! The special protective quality of this particular variety of the stone recommends its use as a talisman for anyone whose living is made on the sea (or other waters), as it is thought to protect from drowning.

It's a Man Thing

Time to make 45 minutes • **Ease of making** 4 • **Length** 23cm (9in)

Men tend to get a little neglected in the jewellery department, so to partly address the balance, here is an idea for an item that is eminently suitable for masculine taste. The bracelet, which is simple to make, could easily be made longer by extending the plaiting (braiding) so that it could be worn as a necklace.

INGREDIENTS

- 1 large variegated jasper bead, 45 x 25mm
- 1 silver-plated trigger clasp
- 2 sterling silver crimp beads
- 2 silver-plated box calottes
- 2 silver-plated jump rings
- 8cm (3in) length of nylon-coated wire
- 3 x 40cm (16in) lengths of 1mm waxed cotton cord, 1 black, 2 brown

1 Using the large jasper bead and the nylon-coated wire, follow Steps 1 and 2 of Down to Earth (see page 77 and above). Using the three lengths of cotton cord, follow Step 4 above, but on one side of the bead there should be two lengths of the cord, so three lengths of cord are threaded through the wire loops. Slide the bead to the centre of the three lengths of cord.

2 Decide on the length you need for your bracelet and then on each side of the bead plait (braid) the three lengths of cord together to the length required. Trim the spare cord and apply a box calotte to either end of the bracelet. Attach a jump ring to each of the box calottes and the trigger clasp to one of the jump rings (see Using Thong or Cord with Box Calottes and Jump Rings, page 16).

Galaxy Drops

Time to make 2 hours • **Ease of making** 3 • **Length** 46cm (18in), plus 8cm (3in) drops

The large beads in this necklace are beautifully glossy galaxy jasper. The drops, which hang haphazardly with a fluid movement, are suspended on nylon-coated wire.

I have chosen to use a matching green gimp in this necklace, but as this is not always easy to obtain, you could substitute it with 'gold' gimp.

Green jasper is associated with rain, but it also has other reputed attributes, among which is that as a healing talisman it can confer a sympathetic nature, bring peaceful sleep and protect from bad dreams.

INGREDIENTS

- 40cm (16in) string of galaxy jasper oval beads, 17 x 13mm
- 42 gold-plated thin rondel beads, 3mm
- 18 gold-plated faceted bicone beads, 3mm
- 10 goldfill plain rondel beads, 3mm
- 1 small packet of faceted bugle beads, 2mm
- a few black large rocaille beads
- 14 goldfill beads, 2mm
- 10 gold-plated bead caps, 6mm
- 1 gold-plated toggle clasp
- 17 goldfill crimp beads
- 7 x 8mm (⅜in) lengths of green gimp
- 56cm (22in) length of nylon-coated wire
- 5 x 20cm (8in) lengths of nylon-coated wire

1 Using one of the 20cm (8in) lengths of nylon-coated wire, gimp and crimp beads, make up the central pair of drops as shown in the photograph (see Using Nylon-coated Wire with Gimp and Crimp Beads, pages 15 and 17).

2 Repeat Step 1 to make the other four sets of drops. The style is meant to be random and so that the drops hang in a very roughly graduated sequence, so don't worry too much about following the exact numbers of small beads. You could also make your drops longer or shorter than those shown.

3 Make up the main body of the necklace, threading on the drops in the appropriate places, using the photograph as a guide to threading and following the instructions for Using Nylon-coated Wire with Gimp and Crimp Beads, page 15.

Jasper is an ideal material for carving and a virtual menagerie of jasper animals are easily available as well as moons stars and other shapes.

Labradorite & Moonstone

These two stones are both feldspars, which makes up around 50 per cent of the Earth's crust. However, don't expect to find the two types seen here just lying in the dust beneath your feet!

In appearance, labradorite is the most striking of the two stones, and to those who use stones for 'magical' reasons, it is often known as 'the temple of the stars'. Both labradorite and moonstone are symbolic of the moon and reputed to enhance our awareness of and attunement to the cycles and rhythms of life. In so doing, they are said to provide the patience to wait for and the intuition to recognize the 'right time'. Labradorite is also linked to the sun and therefore thought to promote vitality and life.

As the moon appears to be a traveller through our heavens and to traverse water safely and affect the tides, so, too, is moonstone believed to ensure safety for those who cross the sea or swim in its waters, making it the ideal gift for sailors and swimmers. Those who wear the moon's namesake stone are thought to benefit from a natural acceptance of the biological rhythms of life and to suffer fewer problems with menstruation, fertility, childbirth and the menopause, while gardeners who carry a piece in their pocket have been known to produce especially plentiful crops.

Other health benefits of moonstone are reputed to be an improvement in disorders of the digestion and circulation, and an ease from the irritation of insect bites. Labradorite is said to be useful in treating disorders of the brain and also in reducing levels of stress, insecurity, fearfulness and anxiety.

APPEARANCE AND COLOUR
Labradorite: transparent or translucent grey with flashes of brilliant blue; moonstone: clear white or milky with iridescence

AVAILABILITY IN BEAD FORM
Both stones are easily available

COUNTRIES OF ORIGIN
Labradorite: Canada, Finland, Greenland, Russia; moonstone: Australia, India, Sri Lanka

BUYER'S GUIDE

Both stones are fairly high priced but are easy to obtain, although the very best – those that are clear yet exhibit good colour – may be more elusive and also considerably more expensive. Faceted beads usually show more colour than smooth.

Intuition

Time to make 3 hours • **Ease of making** 3 • **Length** 53cm (21in)

If labradorite gives us intuition, then this necklace should provide it in spades, as there are so many beads to be threaded! A plead to beginners in beading – don't turn the page! This necklace is not as difficult to make as it looks; the main 'skills' you will need are patience and good eyesight.

Most of the beads are labradorite, but to enhance their blue effect, I have added a few blue-dyed moonstone beads. These may not be easily available, but you can substitute any suitably blue 4mm beads.

The large silver beads will be difficult for you to replicate exactly, as I purchased them from a souk in Egypt. However, any metal bead of a similar size would be just as good, but you must bear in mind that four strands of nylon-coated wire will need to pass through the holes, so make sure that they are large enough. The barrel bead has an extremely large hole, so to prevent the smaller beads from sliding inside, I have placed a 9mm 'silver' bead at either end, but you may not need to do this if you find a barrel bead with a smaller hole.

Moonstone is one of the birthstones for those with a Cancer star sign, while labradorite is suitable for Scorpios.

INGREDIENTS

- 1 large-holed labradorite barrel bead, 35 x 25mm
- 86cm (34in) string of tumble-chip labradorite beads
- 40cm (16in) string of labradorite beads, 4mm
- 40cm (16in) string of dyed blue beads, 4mm
- 2 silver-plated beads, 20mm
- 2 silver-plated oval beads, 10 x 7mm
- 2 'silver' beads, 9mm (at either end of the barrel bead)
- 64 silver-plated rondel beads, 4mm
- 1 silver-plated toggle clasp
- 8 inexpensive crimp beads for use as temporary 'stoppers'
- 2 sterling silver crimp beads
- 4 x 64cm (25in) lengths of fine nylon-coated wire

1 Using pliers, squeeze an inexpensive crimp bead onto one end of one of the lengths of nylon-coated wire. Thread about 16cm (6½in) of the small beads randomly onto the wire in 'blocks' of three to ten and with a rondel bead between each 'block'. Thread through one of the large silver beads and then about 2.5cm (1in) of smaller beads. Thread on one of the 9mm beads, the large labradorite barrel bead and the other 9mm bead. Thread on 2.5cm (1in) of small beads and the remaining large silver bead. Complete the threading of this side of the necklace roughly to match the other side. Apply another temporary crimp bead to the end of the wire.

2 Repeat Step 1 with the other three lengths of nylon-coated wire.

3 When the threading is complete, check that all the lengths of threaded wire are equal – remove the temporary crimp beads and adjust by removing or adding beads.

4 At either end of the strands, thread the four wires through one of the silver-plated oval beads and, treating the lengths of wire as one, use the sterling silver crimp beads to attach the clasp (see Using Nylon-coated Wire with Crimp Beads, page 14).

Heavenly Blue

Time to make 10 minutes • **Ease of making** 1 • **Length** 48cm (19in), plus 4cm (1½in) pendant

As an antidote to the foregoing project, here is something extremely simple and quick to make! The labradorite pendant is ready-made and similar items are relatively easy to obtain, although the best are not cheap. This one has a fabulous blue sheen and is set in heavyweight sterling silver.

The cord on which the item is threaded is from a local haberdashery shop, and you may well find that a search through a similar shop is a rewarding source of unusual cords for pendant-style necklaces.

As the necklace is so simple, no ingredient list or instructions are given, but refer to the instructions for Using Thong or Cord with Box Calottes and Jump Rings, page 16, for finishing the ends of the cord.

Moonbeam

Time to make 2 hours • **Ease of making** 5 • **Length** 49cm (19in)

In times past, man regarded the moon as a magical entity and so, too, has its namesake stone been revered. Take a close look at some of these beads to see how the stone came by its evocative name; there you will see the pearly opalescence, known as schiller, which is reminiscent of the glow of the moon on a clear night. The variety of moonstone in this necklace is less transparent than some other examples, but it still exhibits the same opalescence and, caught in the right light, each bead has a beautiful bluish rainbow sheen.

Because the necklace is knotted, it has a good drape and the beads are protected from loss if the thread should break.

1 Using the largest moonstone bead and the headpin, make up the pendant drop as shown in the photograph and attach it to the bail (see Using Headpins, page 16).

2 Stiffen the beading thread with superglue (see page 15). Make up the necklace using the photograph as a guide to threading, threading on the pendant drop in the centre, and following the instructions for Using Beading Thread with Clamshell Calottes, page 15, and those on page 59 for knotting between the beads.

INGREDIENTS

- 40cm (16in) string of moonstone beads
- a few black small rocaille beads
- 22 silver-plated bead caps, 3mm
- 1 silver-plated bail
- 1 silver-plated toggle clasp
- 1 silver-plated headpin
- 2 silver-plated clamshell calottes
- 86cm (34in) length of beading thread
- bottle of liquid superglue

Night Sky

Time to make 1½ hours • **Ease of making** 3 • **Length** 51cm (20in), plus 8cm (3in) drop

This necklace acquired its name because the flashy colour sheen of the beads reminds me of the clear blue sky seen just above the horizon at the fall of night, with the drops being the sparkle of the brightest stars. The spectacular colour of these beads is enhanced by the faceting of the surface, which reflects light from many angles.

Five large beads were left over after making this necklace, so you could also make a pair of matching earrings. The 4mm beads were a few that remained after designing Intuition (see page 81). Therefore, if you are making only this necklace, you may not want to purchase a whole string when so few are required, in which case you could use almost any other 4mm beads of a toning colour with little detriment to the appearance of the necklace.

To make the necklace, use the photograph as a guide to threading and follow the instructions for Using Nylon-coated Wire with Crimp Beads, page 14, and Using Nylon-coated Wire with Gimp and Crimp Beads, page 15. Note that for the drops, I have applied a crimp bead to the top of each set of beads to hold them in place.

INGREDIENTS

- ✧ 40cm (16in) string of faceted labradorite beads, 13 x 10mm
- ✧ 14 labradorite beads, 4mm
- ✧ 46 gold-plated star-shaped rondel beads, 6mm
- ✧ 19 teal-coloured bugle beads, 3mm
- ✧ 14 gold-plated thin rondel beads, 3mm
- ✧ 7 goldfill oval beads, 5 x 3mm
- ✧ 5 gold-plated bead caps, 4mm
- ✧ 1 gold-plated toggle clasp
- ✧ 12 'gold' crimp beads
- ✧ 2 x 8mm (⅜in) lengths of 'gold' gimp
- ✧ 64cm (25in) length of nylon-coated wire
- ✧ 5 x 12cm (4¾in) lengths of 'gold' nylon-coated wire

It is believed that the magical powers of moonstone and labradorite wax and wane with the moon, so that at full moon they have the most powerful influence and when the moon is waning the least potency.

Lapis Lazuli

Lapis lazuli has been prized by man for thousands of years and has probably been traded as a valuable commodity ever since it was first discovered. Consequently, for around 6,000 years man has toiled at Afghanistan's famous Sar-e-Sang mountain mine to fulfil the demand for this glorious royal blue stone.

A look into history reveals that many past civilizations valued lapis lazuli, but it was the Ancient Egyptians who seemed to especially prize the stone. For the pharaohs, lapis became the blue of the sky for their after-life, its rich colour providing the pigment required for the star-studded heavens in their burial chamber ceilings. In life, too, lapis was treasured and worn in jewellery or formed into protective amulets in the belief that the stone held protective magical powers.

Today, lapis lazuli remains valuable and is much sought after for its vibrant colour. Indeed, the name of the stone has given us the word 'azure' to describe a beautiful blue. The mystical powers of lapis are reputed to be many and varied, among which is the belief that wearing the stone influences and promotes psychic awareness by subduing the conscious mind; that it relieves depression, promotes gentleness, gives courage to the fearful, dispels fantasies, protects children, confers peace and ensures fidelity between lovers.

In respect of healing, lapis lazuli is also considered to be helpful in the treatment of migraine, fevers, respiratory problems, insomnia and depression.

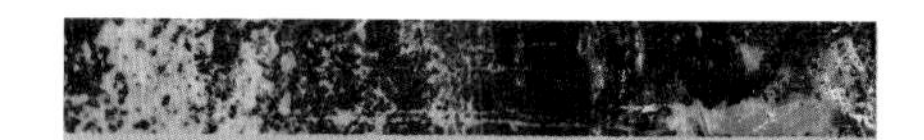

APPEARANCE AND COLOUR
Opaque rich blue often with fleck of pyrites ('fool's gold'); poorer quality with white or grey graining

AVAILABILITY IN BEAD FORM
Relatively common; good-quality beads are expensive

COUNTRIES OF ORIGIN
Afghanistan, Chile, Pamir region of Central Asia, USA

BUYER'S GUIDE

The best lapis lazuli can be expensive, but lesser-quality beads are available at moderate cost. Alternatively, you could use cheaper stones such as sodalite or dyed howlite.

Nefertari

Time to make necklace 3 hours; earrings 30 minutes • **Ease of making** 3 • **Length** necklace 48cm (19in), plus 6.5cm (2½in) drop; earrings 7.5cm (3in)

The stunning blue lapis used in this necklace and earrings set was mined in Afghanistan and the beads, while small, have few flaws in their dense colour.

The design owes its look to a combination of the style of Ancient Egyptian jewellery and my imagination. It is exciting to consider that its namesake Queen Nefertari – renowned for her beautiful tomb, which was only discovered relatively recently – might have worn something similar made from lapis lazuli mined from the same area!

The necklace looks elaborate due to the beautiful gold-plated links, but it is not complicated to make and few skills other than good eyesight and patience are required.

There are no ingredients or instructions for the earrings, as it is easy to see what is required and to make following the instructions for Using Headpins and Multiple Headpins, pages 16–17.

INGREDIENTS

- 4 x 40cm (16in) strings of lapis lazuli tube beads, 3mm
- 75 gold-plated faceted bicone beads, 3mm
- 40 peacock-coloured freshwater pearls
- 17 gold-plated bead caps, 3mm
- 4 gold-plated 3–1 link bars
- 1 gold-plated 5–1 link
- 1 gold-plated toggle clasp
- 15 goldfill crimp beads
- 6 inexpensive crimp beads for use as temporary 'stoppers'
- 2 gold-plated jump rings
- 5 goldfill headpins
- 12 x 8mm (⅜in) lengths of 'gold' gimp
- 6 x 33cm (13in) lengths of nylon-coated wire
- 3 x 5cm (2in) lengths of 'gold' nylon-coated wire

Lapis lazuli is one of the birthstones for three different star signs: Sagittarius, Taurus and Libra.

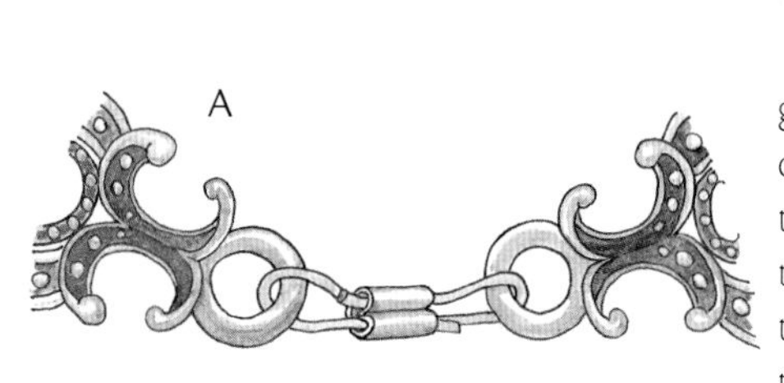

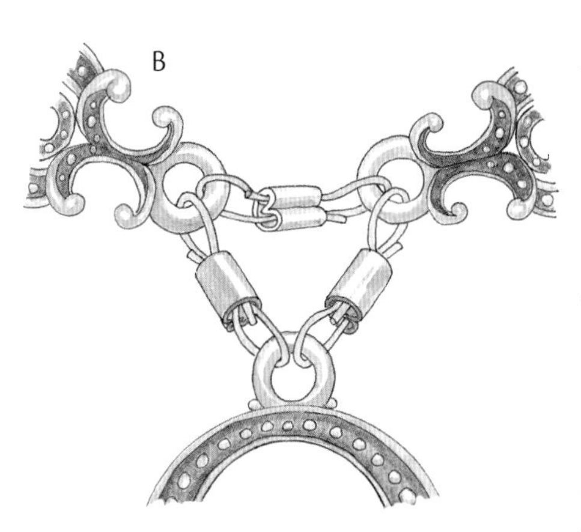

1 Take two of the 3–1 link bars and the 5–1 link and place them before you with three goldfill crimp beads and the three short lengths of nylon-coated wire. Thread one length through the single hole of one of the 3–1 links, then thread on a crimp bead. Thread through the single hole of the other 3–1 link, then thread both ends of the wire back through the crimp bead in different directions. Pull the two ends so that you form a small looped even connection between the two links (diagram A). Use a pair of pliers (preferably special crimp pliers) to squeeze the crimp bead to secure, then trim the spare wire.

2 Using the remaining two short lengths of wire and goldfill crimp beads, follow diagram B to make the other connections between the two 3–1 link bars and the 5–1 link.

3 Attach one of the 33cm (13in) lengths of wire to each of the three holes of one of the 3–1 link bars (see Using Nylon-coated Wire with Gimp and Crimp Beads, page 15). Thread on the beads as shown in the photograph on page 85, then thread the end of each length of wire through the appropriate hole of the other 3–1 link bar. Apply an inexpensive crimp bead to the end of each length of wire (see diagram C). Note that the outer lengths of wire are progressively 6mm (¼in) longer than the inner length. You can achieve this by threading more beads just at the clasp end of each length of wire or by adding more lapis lazuli beads to each sequence.

4 Using the remaining lengths of wire and inexpensive crimp beads, repeat Step 3 for the other side of the necklace.

5 Add the drops to the pendant, using the photograph as a guide to threading and following the instructions for Using Headpins, page 16.

6 Take your necklace to a mirror and hold it up to your neck to make sure that all the lengths of beads hang correctly. After removing the temporary crimp beads, adjust as necessary by adding or removing beads. When you are happy with the result, attach each length to the remaining 3–1 links, as in the first stage of Step 3.

7 Complete your necklace by using the jump rings to attach the clasp (see Using Thong or Cord with Box Calottes and Jump Rings, page 16).

Fortunate travellers to Egypt can't fail to observe that the Egyptians still appear to have a love affair with lapis lazuli, as the souks abound with strings of beads purporting to be lapis. True, the blue necklaces hanging there are beautiful and many are lapis, but others are not, so take care. Also, be aware that the prices, despite bargaining, are generally high, and even after your hard-fought negotiations, you may well be paying more than you would back home!

Poorly coloured lapis lazuli is often dyed to masquerade as a better quality stone.

Royalty

Time to make 1½ hours • **Ease of making** 5 • **Length** 58cm (23in)

Royalty has a simple, almost primitive quality in its plain style and unpolished beads, and I like to think that even hundreds of years from now both the beads and the necklace will have the same appeal as today.

I have chosen an uncluttered look for these beads as, not only are they beautiful to look at, they also have a very tactile finish that would be spoilt by the inclusion of any other large beads. To enhance this tactile quality, I have knotted between each bead, as this always gives free movement to a necklace and has the added advantage of keeping valuable beads safe from loss, should the thread break.

Graduated lengths of disc beads are not common, but any graduated length of beads could be used in this style of necklace.

To make the necklace, use the photograph as a guide to threading and following the instructions for Titania, page 59, for the knotting technique.

Lapis lazuli has long been regarded as the stone of truth and intuition.

INGREDIENTS

- 40cm (16in) string of lapis lazuli discs, graduating from 13–17mm
- 49 gold-plated bead caps, 3mm
- 1 gold-plated thin rondel, 3mm
- 1 gold-plated bail
- 1 gold-plated toggle clasp
- 2 gold-plated clamshell calottes
- 1 goldfill headpin
- 1m (39in) length of beading thread
- bottle of liquid superglue

TIP
When knotting a necklace with small-holed beads, using a thread conditioner helps to ease the thread through the holes without causing it to fray.

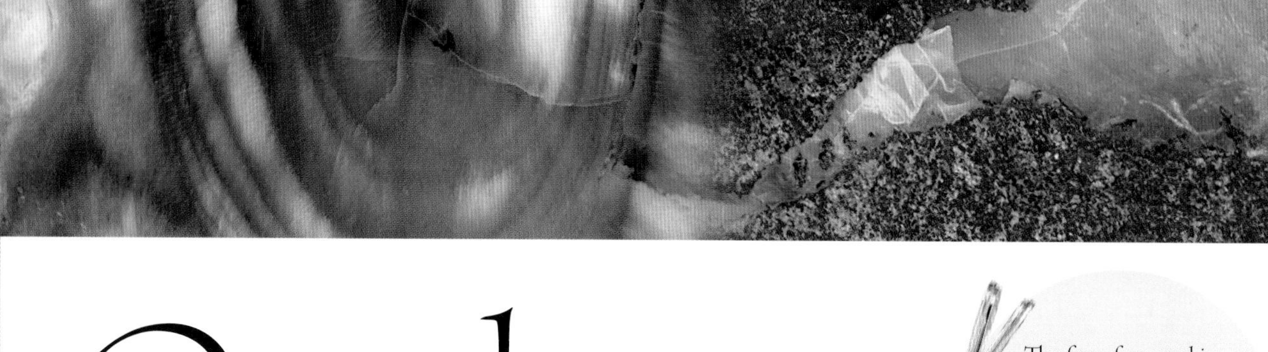

Opal

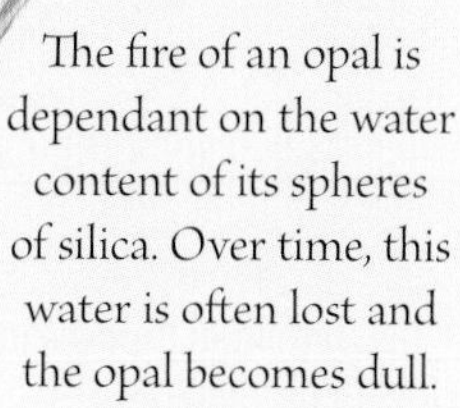

The fire of an opal is dependant on the water content of its spheres of silica. Over time, this water is often lost and the opal becomes dull.

Opal is a mysterious stone of widely varying appearance. It is made up of hydrated silica and as much as a third of its volume may be water. The slice above left is common opal that has invaded and fossilized an ancient tree trunk, while the slice on the right is precious opal in matrix, which exhibits more of the fire and play of colour that we expect from an opal. However, only the very best stones exhibit this quality and normally such stones are not made into beads. Nevertheless, opal beads are available, and this chapter features some of the types that are easy to find. Fiery opal beads are not often seen and are usually quite pale with little colour; they are also very expensive to purchase.

The belief that opal is a stone of misfortune is untrue and originates from a novel by Sir Walter Scott. It is instead considered to be a lucky stone that, among other attributes, enhances psychic awareness, beauty, memory, loyalty and love, as well as attracting wealth. For lovers, opal bestows fidelity and also increases ardour and desire, while encouraging spontaneity.

The following is a fanciful tale of the origins of opal. In times long past, a battle occurred between a rainbow god and a storm god. The rainbow god lost the battle and as a consequence a rainbow fell to the earth and shattered into many pieces to become opal.

For health, opal is reputed to have several benefits, one of which is to instil a strong will to live. It is also believed to cleanse the blood, aid the kidneys, reduce fever and improve eyesight.

APPEARANCE AND COLOUR
Opaque, milky or translucent; white, cream, yellow, blue, red, purple or brown

AVAILABILITY IN BEAD FORM
Non-precious opal easily available, but gem quality more rare, especially in bead form

COUNTRIES OF ORIGIN
Australia, Canada, Mexico, Sardinia, Slovakia, South America, UK, USA

BUYER'S GUIDE

Opal can be an extremely expensive stone and the precious opal is rarely seen in bead form. However, it is easy to find opal beads made from more common types of opal, such as this pink and the Andean blue.

Andean Blue

Time to make 20 minutes • **Ease of making** 3 • **Length** 46cm (18in), plus 3.5cm (1½in) drops

Opal from the Andes contains many shades of blue, pink, beige and black, and the colour seen here is referred to, and sold as, 'blue.' However, in reality it is mainly a minty blue/green shade.

Opal of this colour is reputed to have magical powers that are said to calm the emotions, aid communication and help recovery from colds and flu.

The necklace is easy to make for anyone who has mastered the art of making loops in wire and simply involves using the photograph as a guide to threading and making drops on headpins (see Using Headpins, page 16). Lay the chain flat and untwisted in front of you, then attach each of the drops to the chain with a jump ring (see Using Thong or Cord with Box Calottes and Jump Rings, page 16). Make sure that each drop is attached at regular intervals (I have allowed a gap of six links between each drop) and that they are all attached to the same side of the links on the chain, so that the chain hangs correctly when worn.

This piece of raw opal in matrix demonstrates some of the beautiful play of opal colours.

INGREDIENTS

- 5 faceted oval Andean opal beads, 16 x 12mm
- 4 silver-plated flat square beads with holes from corner to corner, 8mm
- 1 silver-plated diamond-shaped bead, 10 x 8mm
- 5 sterling silver headpins
- 5 sterling silver jump rings
- 46cm (18in) ready-made heavyweight sterling silver chain

Opal is one of the birthstones for Libra and wearing the correct stone for the date of your birth is said to increase its powers.

Briar Rose

Time to make 15 minutes • **Ease of making** 3 • **Length** 1m (39in) maximum

A carved opal flower forms the centrepiece of this very wearable necklace and a little Swarovski crystal hangs loosely in the middle of the flower to give extra interest. Flower beads such as this are available in many different stone types, so you could choose an alternative that may be more suitable for you – for instance, a different birthstone.

The 'cord' on which the necklace is based is faux suede, an imitation that is so good that it had me believing it was the real thing. But unlike real suede, it is made in a multitude of colours, so whatever stone you choose, there is sure to be a faux suede colour to match.

The necklace is of an infinitely variable length as there is no clasp, so it could be worn choker length with the knot and the end drops hanging at the front, or longer with them falling from the back of the neck.

NECKLACE INGREDIENTS

- 1 opal flower, 40mm
- 2 cushion-shaped opal beads, 6 x 4mm
- 1 gold-plated large-holed bead, 8mm
- 3 Swarovski crystal bicone beads, 4mm
- 2 gold-plated thin rondels
- 2 gold-plated bead caps, 5mm
- 1 gold-plated link
- 1 goldfill crimp bead
- 3 gold-plated headpins
- 1 gold-plated jump ring
- 2 gold-plated box calottes
- 2cm (¾in) length of gold-plated gimp
- 4cm (1½in) length of nylon-coated wire
- 1m (39in) length of soft brown faux suede

1 Take the length of nylon-coated wire and thread on the length of gimp, the gold-plated link and the opal flower, followed by the crimp bead. Now thread the other end of the wire through the crimp bead from the opposite direction. Pull the wire ends so that the wire is hidden beneath a loop of gimp (diagram A).

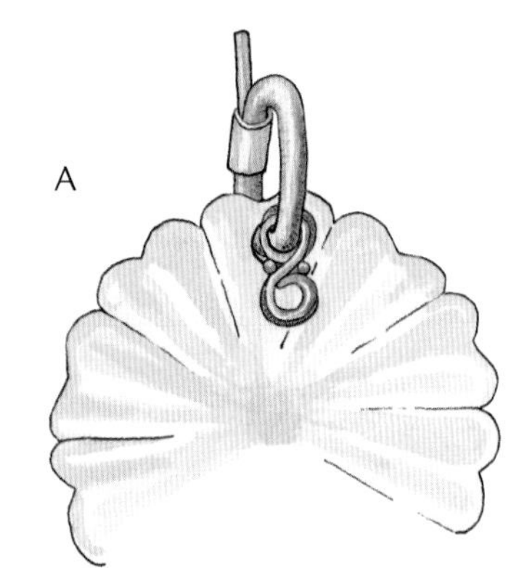

2 Use a pair of pliers to squeeze the crimp bead onto the wire to secure. Use a pair of cutting pliers to trim the wire ends as close as possible to the crimp bead.

3 Thread a Swarovski crystal bead onto a headpin and make a loop (see Using Headpins, page 16). Attach this tiny pendant to the jump ring and then attach this to the lower hole of the link to suspend the bead in the centre of the flower.

4 Thread the length of faux suede through the loop of gimp and slide the flower pendant to the centre of the length. Thread the gold-plated large-holed bead onto both ends of the faux suede together, then slide it down to the loop of gimp.

5 Attach a box calotte to either end of the faux suede (see Using Thong or Cord with Box Calottes and Jump Rings, page 16). Using the photograph as a guide to threading and the instructions for Using Headpins, page 16, make up the two small drops and attach one to each box calotte.

The very best opal, which has an even play of bright colours, may be worth more per carat than diamonds.

Iced Candy

Time to make necklace 1 hour; earrings 30 minutes • **Ease of making** 3 • **Length** necklace 46cm (18in), plus 6.5cm (2½in) drop; earrings 7cm (2¾in)

Pink opal has no fire but instead a soft, satin-like appearance with a delicate feminine colour, which perhaps accounts for its reputation as a stone of love, harmony and peace. It is also regarded as possessing the power of emotional and physical healing. For health, it is said to ease the menopause and skin problems, while alleviating respiratory and heart problems.

When making this necklace, be aware that the shell is a hand-carved natural item and your shell may not be exactly the same as the one shown here, in which case you may need to adjust the number or length of the beaded drops. If you purchase whole strings of beads to make the necklace, you will have plenty left over to make other items, such as the accompanying earrings.

This necklace looks professional and stunning, but any beginner can easily make it. Using the photograph as a guide to threading, make up the drops with the shorter lengths of nylon-coated wire, securing a gimp bead at the lower end, then attach to the shell with gimp and crimp beads following the instructions for Using Nylon-coated Wire with Gimp and Crimp Beads, page 15. The main parts of the necklace are made in the same way. To make the earrings, again use the photograph as a guide to the design and threading, and follow the instructions for Using Headpins, page 16.

Many years ago it was believed that an opal hidden in a folded bay leaf and carried on the person made them invisible!

NECKLACE INGREDIENTS

- 7 baroque faceted oval pink opal beads, about 25 x 13mm
- 20 cushion-shaped opal beads, 10 x 5mm
- 26 cushion-shaped opal beads, 6 x 4mm
- 1 carved mother-of-pearl shell, 10 x 4cm (4 x 1½in)
- 13 gold-plated bead caps, 8mm
- 1 gold-plated cone-shaped bead cap, 8mm
- 20 gold-plated bead caps, 5mm
- 1 gold-plated toggle clasp
- 9 goldfill crimp beads
- 9 x 8mm (⅜in) lengths of 'gold' gimp
- 2 x 25cm (10in) lengths of nylon-coated wire
- 5 x 12cm (4¾in) lengths of nylon-coated wire

EARRINGS INGREDIENTS

- 12 cushion-shaped opal beads, 6 x 4mm
- 8 pink Swarovski crystal bicone beads, 4mm
- 6 goldfill oval beads, 5 x 3mm
- 18 gold-plated thin rondels
- 10 goldfill beads, 2mm
- 2 gold-plated 3–1 links
- 2 gold-plated jump rings
- 8 goldfill headpins
- 1 pair of gold-plated ear-studs

Pearl

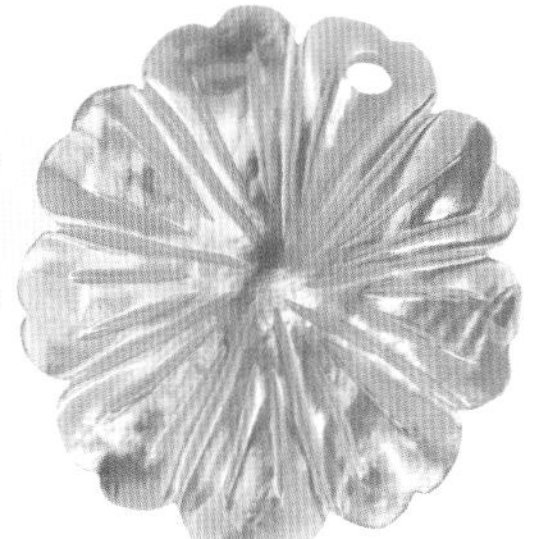

Mother-of-pearl can make a great substitute for pearls, and large, carved sections of shell, such as this flower, are available at low cost.

While pearls are not gemstones, they are certainly considered to be precious gems, and for that reason they deserve their place in this book. For as long as man has used the produce of the sea, the natural pearl has been a source of admiration and curiosity. We can imagine the first find: in the distant past, perhaps a bare-skinned diver sat on the shore with his day's catch of oysters, then, on opening that rare one in a thousand, the slippery contents revealed a perfect pearl within their midst. His face would have lit up with awe, as its purity and lustrous nature must have seemed miraculous. No doubt the unexpected prize would have become a valued treasure. Eventually, so great was the desire for pearls, and so rare the find, that they became unattainable to all but the very wealthy. Consequently, for many years man sought to make acceptable substitutes, and so the cultured, glass and plastic pearl came into being. In relatively recent years, the art of reproducing natural cultured freshwater pearls at relatively low cost has been mastered and now a huge selection of colours, sizes and shapes is available to all.

As may be imagined, such a beautiful item, which appears as a ready-made and perfect gift from nature, has come to symbolize untouched simplicity and, therefore, purity and innocence. It may be for this reason alone that pearls have become the bead of choice for brides; although equally, it could be for their unmistakable lustre that goes so well with bridal wear.

Pearls have fewer attributes than many semi-precious stones, but it is believed that they enhance personal honesty and integrity, confer loyalty and promote the discernment of truth. The wearing of pearls is reputed to help treat nausea and other digestive problems, to improve fertility and also to reduce the pains of childbirth.

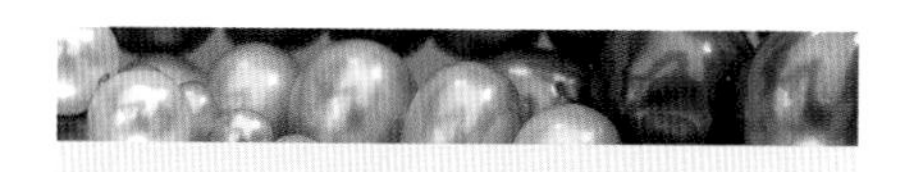

APPEARANCE AND COLOUR
Natural pearls: white, cream, pale pink, iridescent grey; dyed pearls: almost any colour

AVAILABILITY IN BEAD FORM
Natural pearls: very rare; cultured freshwater pearls: common

COUNTRIES OF ORIGIN
Far East

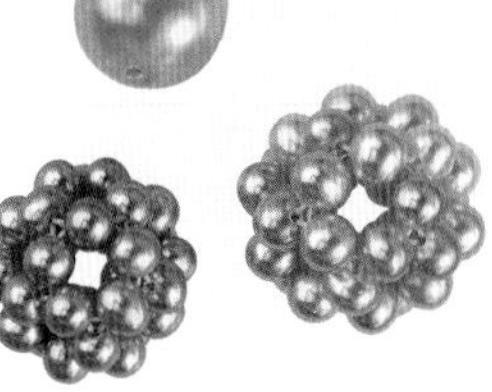

BUYER'S GUIDE

Cultured freshwater pearls are very easy to obtain and vary in price from inexpensive to moderate – the more perfect and lustrous, the higher the price. Artificial pearls are normally very much cheaper.

Party Piece

Time to make 5 hours • **Ease of making** 5
• **Length** 40cm (16in), plus 9cm (3½in) drops

These peacock-coloured 3mm freshwater pearls are not natural in colour, but are dyed to give a dramatic appearance, as in this necklace and earrings set, which is designed for special-occasion wear. There are many such dyed pearls available and this design would look equally good made in natural creamy-coloured pearls for bridal wear.

The necklace requires patience to make, as there are over 630 beads to be threaded, but most people will be able to attempt the project with good results, and the effort spent will be worthwhile. The use of thread conditioner (see page 87) in threading the drops for this necklace and the earrings is almost essential, as the bead holes are so tiny and unconditioned thread will catch and fray very easily.

To make up the earrings, you will need two-thirds of an extra string of pearls as well as eight gold-plated faceted bicone beads and eight bugle beads. The drops are threaded in the same way as those on the necklace, but to enable attachment to the ear-hook, after threading on the first of the two bugles, thread on a crimp bead (and lightly squeeze it to secure in place) and a length of gimp, then thread back through the crimp bead before threading on the next bugle and completing the earring drops.

INGREDIENTS

- 4 x 40cm (16in) strings of freshwater pearls, 3mm
- 20 iridescent twisted bugle beads, 10mm
- 92 gold-plated faceted bicone beads
- 1 gold-plated toggle clasp
- 22 goldfill crimp beads
- 2 x 8mm (⅜in) lengths of 'gold' gimp
- 2m (2¼yd) length of silk beading thread with needle attached
- 2 x 68cm (27in) lengths of fine nylon-coated wire
- thread conditioner

Dark pearls, such as these, are thought to bring luck to the wearer.

1 Treating both lengths of nylon-coated wire as one and using a gimp and a crimp bead, attach one set of ends to one part of the clasp (see Using Nylon-coated Wire with Gimp and Crimp Beads, page 15). Use sharp cutting pliers to trim the spare wire.

2 Thread a gold-plated faceted bicone bead onto both threads together.

3 Thread onto each length of wire three pearls, then onto one length of wire another faceted bicone bead. Now thread the other wire through this last bead from the opposite direction (diagram A).

4 Repeat Step 3 another 14 times. Then for 10 sequences replace the central pearl on the outer side of the necklace with a faceted bicone bead, as shown in the photograph. Continue threading as in Step 3 another 14 times, then thread three more pearls on each length of wire and finish as you started in Steps 1 and 2.

5 Treat your silk thread with the thread conditioner if possible, following the manufacturer's instructions.

6 Tie an overhand knot in the non-needle end of the silk thread, then thread on one goldfill crimp bead and slide it down onto the knot, making sure that both ends of the thread are inside the crimp bead (diagram B). Use pliers (preferably crimp pliers) to gently squeeze the crimp bead over the thread close to the knot, to make sure that it is secure without cutting through the thread.

7 Thread on a gold-plated faceted bicone bead, followed by five pearls, another bicone and a twisted bugle bead. Attach this first drop to the necklace by threading through (from the outer side of the necklace) the first of the 10 central gold-plated faceted bicone beads. Pull the thread through so that the drop hangs loosely but does not reveal too much thread (diagram C).

8 Continue with the same thread to make the next drop, threading on the beads in the same sequence as in Step 7, but in reverse order and increasing the number of pearls threaded by two.

9 Finish off this set of two drops as in Step 6.

10 Repeat Steps 6–9 four more times, each time adding an extra two pearls to create the graduated effect. Then finish the necklace by repeating Steps 6–9 five more times, but this time reducing the pearls on each drop by two. Repeat Step 1 to attach the other part of the clasp.

Moondance

These absolutely gorgeous pearls remind me of a full moon on a summer's night, and they have so much luminescence and subtle colour that the addition of any other beads would detract from their beauty. For this reason, I have simply threaded them on a silk beading thread that matches their soft pink hue and used a plain sterling silver clasp that is set with a garnet cabochon.

To make the necklace, follow the instructions for Titania, page 59, for attaching the clasp using gimp and for the knotting technique.

INGREDIENTS

- 40cm (16in) string of disc-shaped freshwater pearls
- 1 sterling silver toggle clasp
- 2 x 8mm (⅜in) lengths of 'silver' gimp
- 1m (39in) length of silk beading thread with needle attached

Hidden Heart

Time to make 15 hours • **Ease of making** 8 • **Length** 43cm (17in)

Today, a tiara is the perfect adornment to complete the bride's outfit, but many store-bought examples are very expensive, so what better idea than to make your own at a fraction of the cost.

The Hidden Heart tiara is made using only freshwater pearls with a sparkling Swarovski crystal pearl emerging from their midst.

Many tiaras are created on a pre-formed tiara base, and to save yourself some work, you could use one of these for Hidden Heart. However, I prefer to make my own base so that it is both more supple and can also be moulded to the head of the wearer for extra comfort.

Finally, note that this tiara can be reversed and worn at the front of the neck to form a very elaborate pearl collar.

TIP

The Greeks considered that such a rarity as a pearl was caused by a lightning strike, and in India they believed it was caused by a drop of rain being swallowed by an oyster. Other romantic tales have it that the tears of an angel or a drop of dew fell into an open shell where they congealed to create a perfect gem.

INGREDIENTS

- 280 pearls in mixed natural colours and sizes, varying from 3–7mm
- 1 Swarovski crystal heart, 9mm
- 2m (2¼yd) length of fine (28-gauge) wire
- 10m (11yd) length of medium (24-gauge) wire

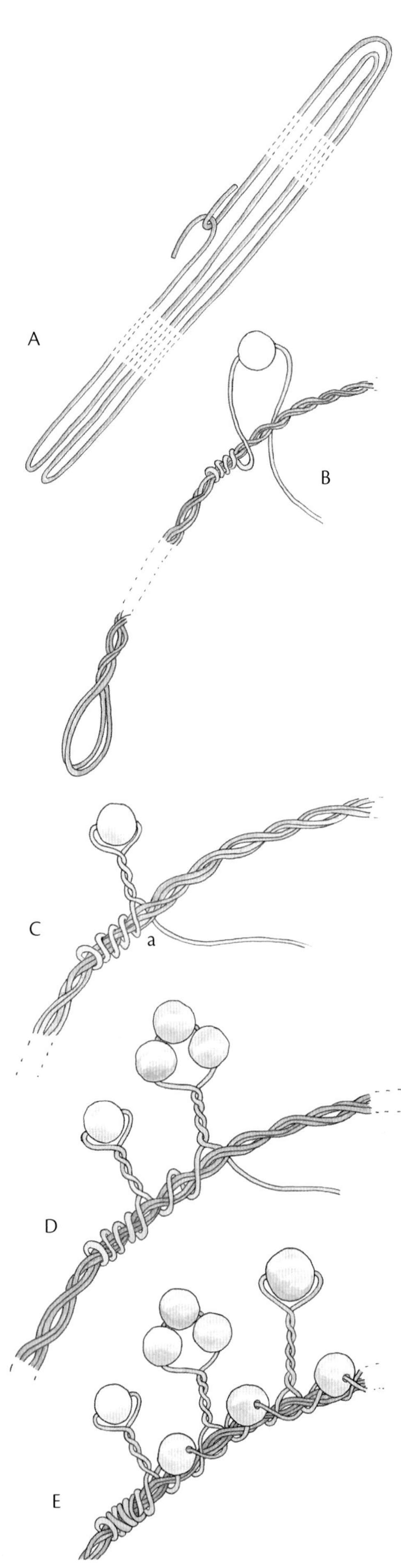

1 Link the two ends of the fine (28-gauge) wire together and twist lightly to secure, then bend into four lengths, with the ends meeting in the centre of one length (diagram A). Please note that if you need your tiara to be on a smaller base, reduce the length of the wire.

2 Hook one end of the four lengths over something secure and strong, like a picture hook on a wall, and then insert a pencil (or something similar) through the loops at the other end and begin twisting the pencil. Keep twisting until all the wires are firmly fixed together in a rope and remain so when you stop twisting. (Be careful as you do this, since, depending on the springiness of the wire, there will be some resistance while twisting and it could spring back and hit you.)

3 When you are satisfied that the wire is thoroughly twisted, form the wire rope into a tiara shape.

4 Cut a 1m (1yd) length of the medium (24-gauge) wire and attach 6cm (2½in) from the end of one side of the tiara base by twisting it around the tiara base. Make sure that the end of the wire is tucked away where it will not be felt when the tiara is worn.

5 When you are satisfied that the wire is secure, thread on a small pearl bead, leaving 1–1.5cm (⅜–⅝in) of straight wire, then bend the wire over and pass the unthreaded length over the other side of the tiara base to the one that it rises from (diagram B).

6 With the thumb and forefinger of one hand holding the tiara base and wires in place at point 'a' of diagram C, use the other hand to grasp the pearl and then twist it so that the bead stands upright on a short length of twisted wire stalk.

7 Wind the wire once around the tiara base and then repeat Steps 5–6. Continue in this way all the way around the tiara, increasing the height of some of the wire stalks as you go and keeping the density of the pearls even and to suit your requirements. As the height of the beaded pearls on the tiara gets greater, introduce some three-bead stalks (diagram D), and remember to add the crystal heart at the top centre of the tiara. Note that as you work you will run out of wire and need to keep using new lengths. Don't be tempted to try and work with long lengths of wire, as it is fine and easily becomes kinked and tangled.

8 When you reach the same point at which you started on the other side of the tiara, it is almost finished, and if you like the appearance, you could leave it as it is. However, here I have added one more threading of pearls that sits immediately against the wire of the tiara base and partially hides it. To do this, attach another length of wire to one end of the base and simply wind the wire in and around the base, threading on small beads as you go (diagram E).

9 Now look at your tiara and check that the beads are evenly distributed; wires can be twisted further and bent to make small adjustments, and if necessary more beads can be added.

Shells such as this one, with incompletely formed pearls, are now available cut and polished to use as pendants.

Purple Night

Time to make necklace 40 minutes; earrings 15 minutes • **Ease of making** necklace 2; earrings 3 • **Length** necklace 48cm (19in); earrings 5cm (2in)

Purple Night is included to showcase one more of the many colours available in freshwater pearls and to demonstrate just how easy and quick it can be for a complete novice to produce a stunning set of jewellery; in less than an hour, even a complete beginner should be able to make both necklace and earrings.

The earrings are suspended on niobium ear-hooks with an anodized colour to match that of the pearls. Niobium ear-hooks are available in about six different colours, so you should be able to choose something that tones with your beads.

To make the necklace, use the photograph as a guide to threading and follow the instructions for Using Nylon-coated Wire with Gimp and Crimp Beads, page 15. For the earrings, again use the photograph as a guide to the design and follow the instructions for Using Headpins and Multiple Headpins, pages 16–17.

TIP
Artificial pearls, which owe nothing to nature, are plentiful, inexpensive and made in many colours, so they could be an alternative for this necklace if you are seeking to save money.

NECKLACE INGREDIENTS

- 40cm (16in) string of purple freshwater pearls, 8–9mm
- 22 gold-plated bead caps
- 10 gold-plated thin star-shaped rondel beads, 7mm
- 2 gold-plated faceted bicone beads, 7mm
- 1 gold-plated toggle clasp
- 2 goldfill crimp beads
- 2 x 8mm (⅜in) lengths of purple gimp
- 58cm (23in) length of nylon-coated wire

EARRINGS INGREDIENTS

- 2 purple freshwater pearls, 8–9mm
- 6 goldfill oval beads, 5 x 3mm
- 4 purple anodized niobium coils, 2mm
- 4 gold-plated bead caps, 4mm
- 4 purple anodized niobium headpins
- 1 pair of purple anodized niobium ear-hooks

A natural pearl is caused by the irritation of something like a grain of sand beneath the shell of an oyster. Today, that 'irritation' is artificially introduced and may be quite a large and pre-shaped item to give us a wide choice of pearl bead shapes, such as hearts or squares.

Pearl is one of the birthstones for both Gemini and Sagittarius.

Peridot

Peridot is a birthstone for both Leo and Libra.

Peridot, which is also known by the names of olivine and chrysolite, has been a prized gemstone for many thousands of years. During the height of the Ancient Egyptian empire, it was excavated almost exclusively from an island in the Red Sea known as 'serpent island', where the source was jealously guarded and all intruders put to death on approach.

One of the main attributes of peridot is protection and in past times it was believed that, for this effect, a peridot bead should be strung on a thread made from the hair of a donkey's tail and worn on the arm!

Emotionally, peridot is supportive and calming; it alleviates rage, envy and resentment, while also combating stress and encouraging confidence. It is also reputed to help the mind by bringing clarity to thoughts, and also to assist in reflecting on past experiences and learning the benefit of them. In similar vein, peridot is said to help with the retrieval of lost possessions.

Peridot is considered to be excellent for promoting physical well-being and acts as a tonic that aids the heart, lungs and digestive system. It is also thought to improve various eyesight problems and a piece placed on the stomach during labour was historically reputed to help ease the pain of contractions!

APPEARANCE AND COLOUR
Clear or opaque and usually small crystals of leaf green

AVAILABILITY IN BEAD FORM
One of the less common stones in bead form

COUNTRIES OF ORIGIN
Brazil, Burma, Egypt, Ireland, Russia, Sri Lanka, USA (Arizona)

BUYER'S GUIDE

Most peridot beads are small, so if you require large beads in this colour, your best option is to use glass beads, such as the glass disc pictured here. Peridot is not among the cheapest semi-precious stone beads, but baroque beads such as those used in the projects are quite reasonable in price.

Spring Green

Time to make 3 hours • **Ease of making** 6 • **Length** 20cm (8in)

The peridot in this bracelet is bursting with the colour of spring with its tracery of newborn green leaves, and I thought that the only element to enhance it was the delicacy of spring flowers. Thus the idea for this bracelet was formed and tiny rocaille beads became the flowers that peep from between the leaves.

Many of these peridot beads have extremely small holes and some beads require a thread to pass through them twice. Therefore, I found a bead reamer to enlarge the holes essential in making this bracelet (see page 13). You may be fortunate and purchase beads with reasonable holes, but if not, you should acquire a bead reamer; it will eventually save its cost in beads that would otherwise be unusable.

One and a half strings of beads are used for the bracelet, and even after making the slide and earrings from the remaining beads, you will have enough left over to make another item of jewellery.

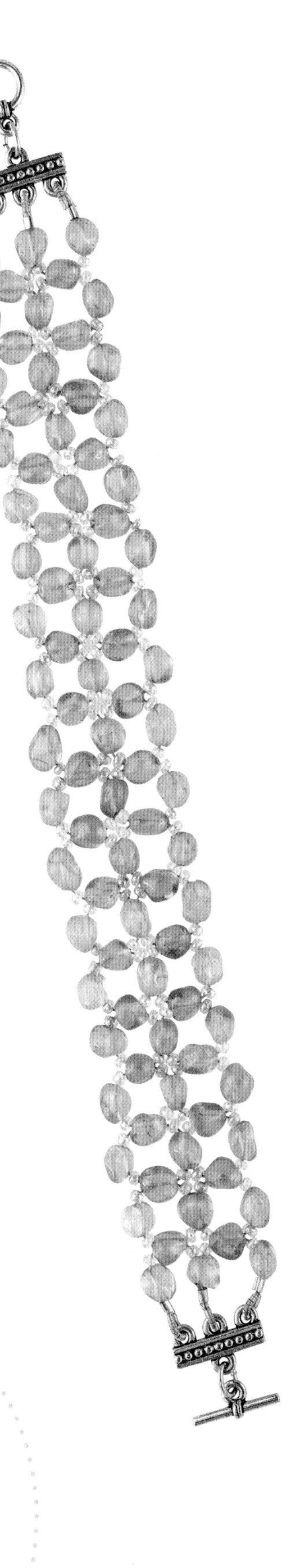

INGREDIENTS

- 2 x 40cm (16in) strings of baroque peridot beads, 6–7mm
- a few small rocaille beads in 3 delicate colours
- 2 gold-plated 3–1 links
- 1 gold-plated toggle clasp
- 6 goldfill crimp beads
- 2 gold-plated jump rings
- 6 x 8mm (⅜in) lengths of green (or 'gold') gimp
- 4 x 51cm (20in) lengths of fine nylon-coated wire.

1 Using the gimp and crimp beads, attach one end of each of the four lengths of nylon-coated wire to the three loops of one of the 3–1 links, attaching two to the central loop but treating them as one (diagram A) (see Using Nylon-coated Wire with Gimp and Crimp Beads, page 15).

2 Thread a peridot bead onto each of the two outside wires and thread another peridot bead onto the central wires together. Then thread a rocaille bead onto each of the four wires.

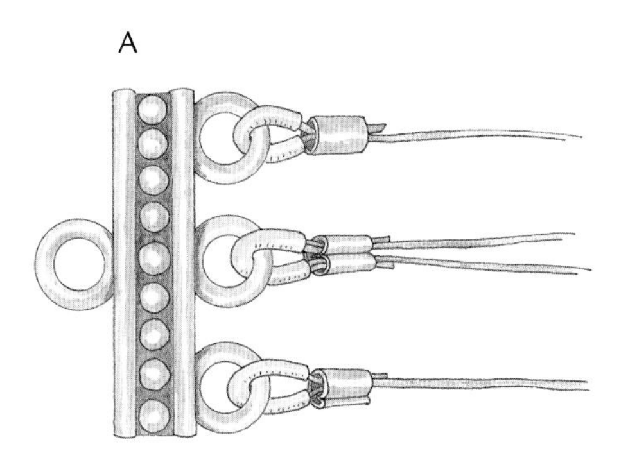

TIP
To make a wider bracelet, use the same method but employ an extra two strands of wire and beads, and attach them to 5–1 links at either end.

3 Thread a peridot bead onto each of the two outside wires, then thread the two inside wires through these last two peridot beads in opposite directions (diagram B).

4 Thread another rocaille bead onto each wire (keep touching rocaille beads the same colour so that they are grouped and resemble little flowers).

5 Repeat Steps 2–4 another 17 times. As you go, keep the wires as even as possible and pulled tightly enough not to show any wire, but not so tight that the bracelet loses its drape and movement.

6 Attach the ends of the beaded wires to the other 3–1 link, as in Step 1, and trim any spare wire.

7 Finish the bracelet by using jump rings to attach the clasp (see Using Thong or Cord with Box Calottes and Jump Rings, page 16).

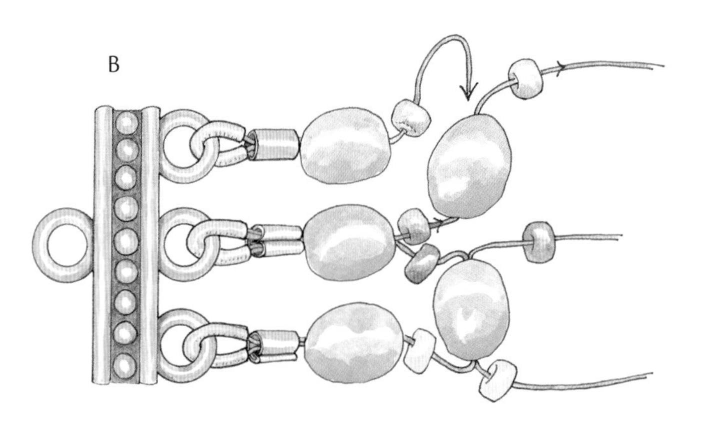

Spring Green Earrings

Time to make 1 hour • **Ease of making** 3 • **Length** 7.5cm (3in)

These delicate earrings have a beautifully fluid movement and may appear difficult to make, but even a beginner can produce this stunning jewellery item within an hour. Just use the photograph as a guide to the design and follow the instructions for Using Headpins and Multiple Headpins, pages 16–17, to form loops in the headpin wire and link them together.

INGREDIENTS

- 18 baroque peridot beads, 6–7mm
- 32 small rocaille beads in 3 delicate colours
- 2 goldfill oval beads, 5 x 3mm
- 10 goldfill headpins (use the leftover trimmings for some of the small links)
- 8 gold-plated jump rings
- 1 pair of green anodized niobium ear-hooks

The ancient Romans wore a ring set with peridot as an antidote to depression.

Spring Green Hair-slide

Time to make 45 minutes • **Ease of making** 4 • **Length** 6cm (2½in)

To complete the Spring Green scene, I have designed a more unusual jewellery item. Blank hair-slides, such as this one, can be purchased in several sizes and make ideal bases on which to thread beads, so when you have tackled this one, why not try another, maybe larger or smaller, or perhaps in pony-tail style. You can use many different combinations of beads to produce hair ornaments that are truly unique and sure to be admired.

INGREDIENTS

- 26 baroque peridot beads, 6–7mm
- about 21 small rocaille beads in 3 delicate colours
- 1 'silver' hair-slide base
- 40cm (16in) length of 'silver' fine jewellery wire

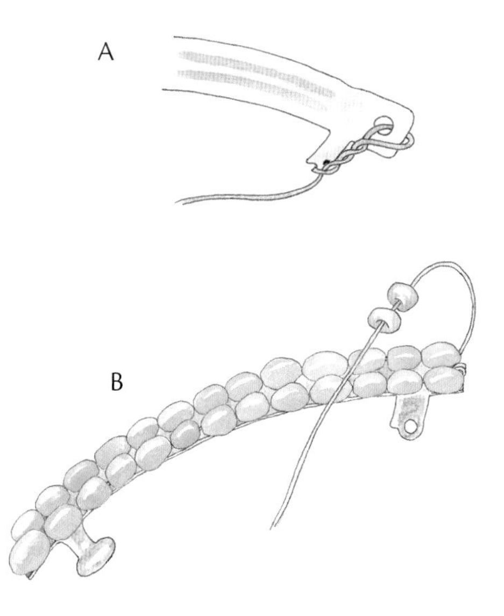

1 Take the hair-slide apart, noting the order in which the three pieces fit together. The beads are threaded onto section 'a' shown in the photograph below, and the length of jewellery wire should be threaded through one hole of this piece and twisted securely to attach (diagram A). (Sections 'b' and 'c' form the 'clasp', and fit at the back of section 'a'.)

2 Thread a length of 13 peridot beads onto the wire, or enough to match the length of your hair-slide, then lay these along the length of the metal bar (section 'a'). At the other end of the bar (section 'a'), thread the wire through the hole and around the end of the bar twice. Thread on another matching length of peridot beads and lay along the bar beside the first length. Secure the wire around the end hole of the bar so that the bar appears as in diagram B.

3 Thread two small rocaille beads onto the wire, then wrap the wire and beads diagonally around the bar, over and between the beads already threaded, making sure that the two rocaille beads are left in the centre to sit between the two strands of peridot and that the wire is hidden from view (diagram B). Continue threading in this way and keep the wire as taut as possible at all times.

4 When you reach the other end of the bar and you are satisfied with the appearance of your hair-slide, finish off by wrapping the wire around one of the holes several times and then tucking the end of the wire out of sight beneath the beads.

5 Reassemble the hair-slide components and it is ready to wear!

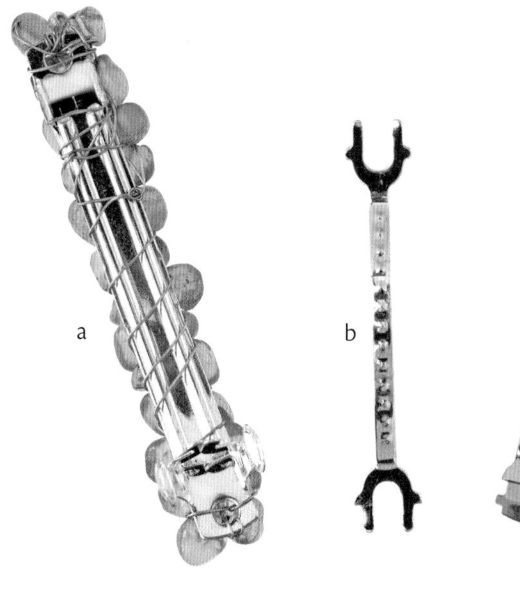

Peridot is believed to attract love and, if worn to bed, promote peaceful, dream-free sleep.

Rose Quartz

Rose quartz is a decorative variety of the same crystal family as amethyst, citrine and rock crystal. All these stones, except rock crystal, were formed in the presence of metallic/mineral impurities and these produce the different colours. In the case of rose quartz, the causative agents are small quantities of titanium or manganese.

Like all crystal stones, rose quartz is very popular and is said to promote beauty, friendship, peace, happiness, love and fidelity. The soft warmth of colour exhibited by rose quartz reflects these gentle 'magical' properties and also ensures that it is a stone worn predominantly by women (sexist maybe, but how many men have you seen wearing pink jewellery?) As a jewellery item for women, the stone is recommended to be worn in a heart shape, when it is reputed to attract love!

Rose quartz is considered to be the finest of all stones for emotional healing, and for physical health it is thought to aid the circulatory system and the lungs, and to relieve vertigo.

A stone of such a feminine hue is obviously ideal as a gift for a baby girl's birth or christening. A simple pendant of perhaps a small heart or delicate teardrop shape, suspended on a sterling silver chain, would make an apt and special present, and could be worn throughout the individual's life. The stone is highly appropriate for brides, too, and combines well with the traditional pearl for bridal jewellery. In both instances, the items are sure to be treasured and could in the future become family heirlooms.

APPEARANCE AND COLOUR
Translucent or clear six-sided crystals in pale pink

AVAILABILITY IN BEAD FORM
Common

COUNTRIES OF ORIGIN
Brazil, India, Japan, Madagascar, South Africa, USA

BUYER'S GUIDE

Rose quartz is very easy and inexpensive to purchase, and in many instances will cost less than the equivalent size in glass beads. It is available in a multitude of small and large, plain and shaped beads.

Rosebud

Time to make necklace 1½ hours; earrings 30 minutes • **Ease of making** 3 • **Length** necklace 43cm (17in), plus 5cm (2in) drop; earrings 6cm (2½in)

Rosebud necklace and earrings are so delicate in appearance that they look almost fragile, but the beads used won't damage easily, and the strands of tiny beads on the necklace are threaded on nylon-coated wire for extra strength.

When purchasing semi-precious stone beads, such as these, it is not always possible to find beads of exactly the same size and style as those in the projects; for instance, your teardrop or flower beads may vary from those featured here. However, similar beads of the same stone type are usually available so that you can create a necklace with a slightly different look.

Both items could appear complicated to the beading beginner, but they are quite easy to make, and all the techniques required are to be found in Using Nylon-coated Wire with Gimp and Crimp Beads, page 15, for the necklace, and Using Headpins, page 16, for the earrings. To make up the necklace, thread the strands of small beads first and attach them to jump rings. They should then be threaded on in the correct position while threading the main part of the necklace. When making the earrings, first make up each teardrop bead on a headpin. In that way, the drops will be ready to thread on in the correct position while threading the strand of smaller beads.

NECKLACE INGREDIENTS

- ✧ 40cm (16in) string of rose quartz teardrop beads, 13 x 9mm
- ✧ 9 rose quartz flower beads, 12mm
- ✧ 40cm (16in) string of rose quartz beads, 2mm
- ✧ 24 gold-plated thin rondel beads, 4mm
- ✧ 14 goldfill beads, 2mm
- ✧ 1 gold-plated toggle clasp
- ✧ 6 goldfill crimp beads
- ✧ 4 gold-plated jump rings
- ✧ 6 x 8mm (⅜in) lengths of 'gold' gimp
- ✧ 53cm (21in) and 12cm (4¾in) lengths of nylon-coated wire
- ✧ 32cm (12½in) length of fine nylon-coated wire

EARRINGS INGREDIENTS

- ✧ 2 rose quartz teardrop beads, 13 x 9mm
- ✧ 28 rose quartz beads, 2mm
- ✧ 8 goldfill oval beads, 5 x 3mm
- ✧ 4 gold-plated thin rondel beads, 4mm
- ✧ 2 gold-plated 2–1 links
- ✧ 4 goldfill crimp beads
- ✧ 2 gold-plated headpins
- ✧ 2 gold-plated jump rings
- ✧ 1 pair of gold-plated ear-studs
- ✧ 1 pair of clutch backs for ear-studs
- ✧ 2 x 10cm (4in) lengths of fine nylon-coated wire

Handbag Charmer

Time to make 1 hour • **Ease of making** 3 • **Length** 16cm (6½in)

Beads are so popular today that they have even found their way onto our handbags, and surely no one can have failed to notice the trend for handbag charms. So I thought I would show you how to make your own. Alternatively, you could scale down the size and make a beaded key charm. Each member of the family could have their own version of key charm made with stones to suit their birth date.

To add interest to this handbag charm, I have used additional beads made from glass, bone, ceramic, wood and fibre-optic glass, but you can use any beads you like and this is a good opportunity to use up oddments.

TIP
Remember always to open and close jump rings sideways or their strength will be lost.

INGREDIENTS

- ✧ 8 rose quartz beads, mixed sizes and shapes
- ✧ 8 additional large beads
- ✧ 14 small beads, mainly gold with 1 wooden and 1 rocaille bead
- ✧ 1 gold-plated large box calotte
- ✧ 8 gold-plated small box calottes
- ✧ 16 gold-plated headpins
- ✧ 8 gold-plated jump rings
- ✧ 4 x 6–8cm (2½–3in) lengths of 1mm waxed cotton cord in 2 colours
- ✧ 1 'gold' key-ring

Rose quartz is often colour-enhanced or strung on deep pink or red thread to give it a deeper and more attractive colour.

1 Secure the large box calotte to the ends of all four lengths of cotton cord (see Using Thong or Cord with Box Calottes and Jump Rings, page 16). Trim the cords so that each is a different length to the others.

2 Secure a small box calotte to the other end of each length of cord, then secure another small box calotte near the centre of each length of cord with the loops of the calotte hanging downwards (diagram A).

3 Use the headpins to make small beaded drops as shown in the photograph (see Using Headpins, page 16). Attach two unmatched drops to each jump ring and then attach a jump ring to each small box calotte loop.

4 Open the jump ring of the key-ring and attach it to the loop of the large box calotte to complete the charm.

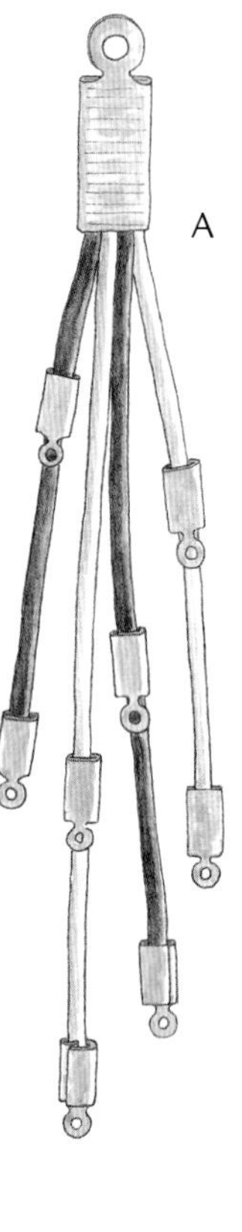

Lily Rose

Time to make 1 hour • **Ease of making** 3 • **Length** 21cm (8¼in)

Using a few of the same beads as seen in Rosebud (see page 103), Lily Rose is a delightful bracelet with great feminine appeal for summertime wear. The rose quartz beads are disc shaped and carved to give the appearance of a flower, and here I have spaced them well apart so that their individual charm is more apparent.

The lily spacer bars have great quality and are of superb design, but silver-plated items such as these tend to tarnish easily, especially when not worn regularly. It is, therefore, a good idea to store silver or silver-plated jewellery in a small polythene bag. This ensures that they are in a dry atmosphere and helps the silver keep its bright colour.

INGREDIENTS

- ✧ 4 rose quartz flower beads, 12mm
- ✧ 5 silver-plated 2-hole spacer bars, 15 x 10mm
- ✧ 10 silver-plated rondel beads, 4mm
- ✧ 20 silver-plated bead caps, 3mm
- ✧ a few pink rocaille beads
- ✧ 1 silver-plated toggle clasp
- ✧ 2 crimp beads
- ✧ 2 silver-plated clamshell calottes
- ✧ 2 x 28cm (11in) lengths of nylon-coated wire.

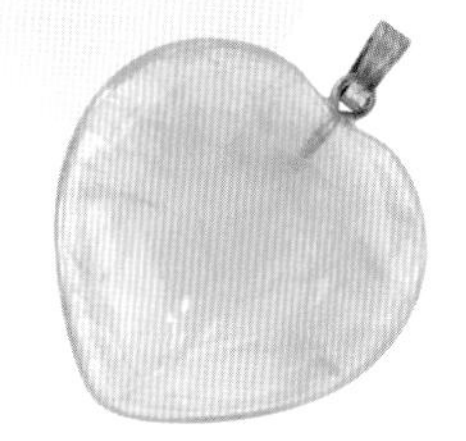

Rose quartz – the gentle love crystal.

1 Secure a crimp bead to one end of the two lengths of nylon-coated wire together, then thread the two wires through the hole of a clamshell calotte so that the crimp bead sits inside the 'shell' of the calotte, trim any spare wire and close the calotte (see Using Nylon-coated Wire with Crimp Beads and Clamshell Calottes, page 15).

2 Thread one rondel bead onto both wires together and then thread four small rocaille beads and a bead cap onto each wire. Thread each wire through one of the holes of a 2-hole spacer bar.

3 Thread onto each of the wires one bead cap and four rocaille beads, then thread both wires through a rondel bead and then a rose quartz bead.

4 Repeat Steps 2–3 until all the beads are threaded, then make any necessary adjustments before attaching to the remaining clamshell calotte, as in Step 1. Finish the bracelet by attaching one part of the toggle clasp to each calotte loop.

Rose quartz is one of the birthstones for Virgo and Taurus, so would make an ideal gift for a female friend with an appropriate birthday.

Ruby

In the Middle Ages, a king of Ceylon who was over 90 years of age was reputed to keep his youthful looks by rubbing a beautiful ruby over the skin of his face every day.

Ancient Hindus called ruby 'the king of stones' and believed that it held an inextinguishable flame, and even today, in its highest quality, it is regarded as the most valuable of the three true precious gemstones, with diamond and sapphire being the other two.

Ruby occurs in several places in the world and in these countries it may, in the appropriate areas, be found in the gravel deposits of rivers. Imagine the excitement of finding a perfect uncut ruby in tumbling waters, where washed from their rocky origins it might lie among the pebbles, protected by its extreme hardness from damage by other stones.

The magical attributes of ruby are many and the stone is considered to be very powerful. At one time it was believed to conserve the body heat of the wearer and that if cast into water it had the power to cause it to boil! It was also thought that the owner of a brilliant ruby would have a peaceful life and that his home, land and crops would be protected from storms and other dangers. For it to be effective, however, the ruby should be set into a ring or bracelet and worn on the left side.

Today, ruby is still reputed to protect from both physical and mental ill-health, and the stone is said to dispel unhappiness, improve willpower and confidence, increase loving emotions, bestow gentleness and bring peaceful sleep, as well as to protect the body from fevers, heart trouble and toxins, and the home from damage by storms. It is also considered to be a wealth-attracting stone, bringing business success and good fortune. Indeed, dreaming of a ruby is said to predict future success. For a business person this could mean monetary gain, while for a gardener the 'success' could be an abundant harvest.

APPEARANCE AND COLOUR
Opaque, translucent or clear red crystals

AVAILABILITY IN BEAD FORM
Rare, and even unpolished drilled crystal beads are expensive

COUNTRIES OF ORIGIN
Afghanistan, Burma, Cambodia, India, Kenya, Madagascar, Mexico, Sri Lanka, Thailand

BUYER'S GUIDE

Ruby in bead form is very expensive and you may wish to use glass substitutes, such as the Swarovski crystal beads pictured far right or the oval glass bead seen below.

High Summer

Time to make 1 hour • **Ease of making** 3 • **Length** 46cm (18in), plus 4cm (1½in) drop

Ruby beads are expensive, but if you want the real thing without its costly price tag, there is an alternative: ruby with zoisite, the oval beads seen here. This stone has additional benefits to those listed for ruby and among these it is said to promote the ability to remain part of 'the crowd,' while retaining a strong individuality.

The beads that I have used are predominantly green, but a closer look reveals ruby crystals. They reminded me of the deep greens and pinky reds of high summer, hence the name. The pendant is pure ruby. It is obviously not a high-quality stone and was inexpensive; similar polished crystals are fairly easily obtained.

The necklace is easily made using the photograph as a guide to threading and following the instructions for Using Nylon-coated Wire with Gimp and Crimp Beads, page 15. The pendant is formed by using epoxy glue to fix the bail to the polished stone.

INGREDIENTS

- 1 ruby polished stone, about 35 x 30mm
- 40cm (16in) string of ruby with zoisite beads, 10 x 8mm
- 10 Swarovski crystal bicone beads, 6mm
- 10 Swarovski crystal bicone beads, 4mm
- 30 frosted green large rocaille beads
- 22 ruby-coloured medium rocaille beads
- 2 gold-plated rondel beads, 5mm
- 22 gold-plated bead caps, 3mm
- 20 gold-plated faceted bicone beads, 3mm
- 2 goldfill beads, 2mm
- 1 gold-plated leaf bail
- 1 gold-plated trigger clasp
- 1 gold-plated jump ring
- 2 goldfill crimp beads
- 56cm (22in) length of nylon-coated wire
- epoxy glue

Ruby Drops

Time to make 30 minutes • **Ease of making** 4 • **Length** 12cm (4¾in)

The rubies in these earrings are real and are fairly typical of those that you might find in the cheapest ruby bead strings. These, however, were purchased more or less as you see them, but instead of being earrings, they started their jewellery life as part of a sterling silver chain necklace. To make the earrings, I cut the necklace up into appropriate lengths and at the end of each drop of chain added one extra ruby (taken from leftover sections of chain). I then merely added sterling silver ear-hooks to complete this stunning pair of dangly earrings. No list of ingredients is given, as they can so obviously be seen in the photograph.

Sapphire & Iolite

The rare and precious stone that we all know as sapphire is a variety of the extremely hard mineral corundum and is a close relative of ruby. The beautiful blue colour that we are all familiar with is produced during its formation by the presence of iron and titanium.

As might be expected from a stone of such beauty, sapphire has long been treasured and man has prized it for its appearance alone. However, as with all natural stones, over the years meanings and powers have been ascribed to sapphire and it has become recognized as an item with a beauty more than 'skin deep'. The attributes of sapphire are numerous and it is said to promote kindness, compassion, joy, truth, sincerity, psychic awareness, peace, lightness of spirit, depth of thought and enhanced understanding. It is also said to be a protective stone, which guards the wearer from ill-health, envy, anger, fraud, poison and captivity. For healing purposes, sapphire has acquired a reputation for strengthening the eyes and relieving fevers and nose bleeds.

Everyone knows that sapphire is expensive and therefore beyond the reach of most people, so the projects in this chapter are made from a stone called iolite (or water sapphire). In reality, this bears no relationship to sapphire and has its own attributes. Among these are a reputed ability to aid clear understanding and self-expression, while also protecting from drunkenness and alleviating headaches.

APPEARANCE AND COLOUR
Clear, translucent or opaque; blue, purple, pink, yellow and black

AVAILABILITY IN BEAD FORM
Quite rare and very expensive

COUNTRIES OF ORIGIN
Australia, Brazil, India, Kenya, Myanmar, Sri Lanka

Tanzanite is often used as a substitute for sapphire.

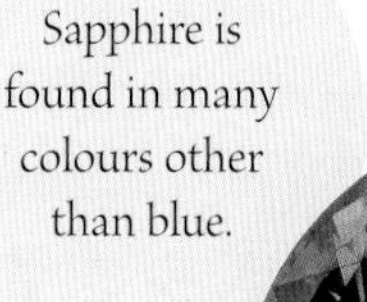

Sapphire is found in many colours other than blue.

BUYER'S GUIDE

As sapphire beads are very expensive, you may wish to use a cheaper stone such as iolite. However, iolite beads are rarely above 4mm in size, so if you need larger beads, Swarovski crystal would make a good alternative.

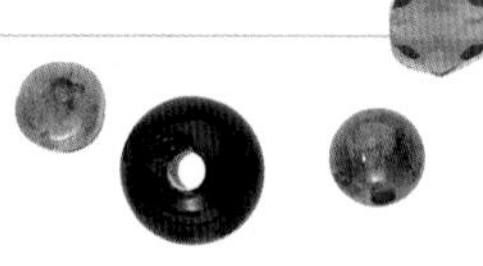

Ripples

Time to make bracelet 2 hours; earrings 30 minutes
• **Ease of making** bracelet 4; earrings 3
• **Length** bracelet 20cm (8in); earrings 5cm (2in)

This delicate bracelet uses about two-thirds of a string of iolite beads. Attach the two wires to the clasp with gimp and crimp beads, following the instructions for Using Nylon-coated Wire with Gimp and Crimp Beads, page 15, then thread on the beads as shown in the photograph, with the two wires travelling through the goldfill oval beads from opposite directions (diagram A). Keep the wires evenly taut, but not pulled too tight.

The earrings, using the same iolite beads and other beads used for the bracelet and Midnight, can be made following the instructions for Using Nylon-coated Wire with Gimp and Crimp Beads, pages 15 and 17.

Sapphire is a birthstone for Taurus and Gemini.

A

BRACELET INGREDIENTS

- 68 iolite beads, 4mm
- 32 goldfill oval beads, 5 x 3mm
- 2 goldfill crimp beads
- 1 goldfill jump ring
- 1 goldfill trigger clasp
- 2 x 8mm (⅜in) lengths of 'gold' gimp
- 2 x 46cm (18in) lengths of fine nylon-coated wire

Midnight

Time to make 2 hours • **Ease of making** 3 • **Length** 46cm (18in)

This necklace looks a million dollars, but once again is inexpensive to make. Just six beads more than a complete string of iolite are used, or just the one string without the back drops. The glass beads are available in a vast range of sizes, to match any semi-precious stone.

First prepare all the graduated drops by threading the beads in the sequence shown in the photograph onto the headpins and following Using Headpins, page 16, to form loops in the headpin wire. To make the main string, using gimp and crimp beads, attach the wire to the clasp (see Using Nylon-coated Wire with Gimp and Crimp Beads, page 15), then thread on the beads as shown, threading on the drops in sequence as you go. If the back drops are required, thread beads as shown onto the remaining headpins and suspend from the ring part of the clasp.

INGREDIENTS

- 40cm (16in) string of iolite beads, plus 6 for the back drops, 4mm
- 87 Czech glass faceted beads, 3mm
- 18 goldfill oval beads, 5 x 3mm
- 48 goldfill beads, 2mm
- 16 gold-plated rondel beads, 5mm
- 1 gold-plated toggle clasp
- 18 goldfill headpins
- 2 'gold' crimp beads
- 2 x 8mm (⅜in) lengths of 'gold' gimp
- 56cm (22½in) length of nylon-coated wire

Sodalite

Sodalite is one of the birthstones for Sagittarius.

Sodalite is a similar but less bright blue than its close cousin lapis lazuli, and as it is less expensive, it could be used as a colour substitute. One of the main differentiating features between the two stones is a lack of pyrites (or 'fool's gold' – a brassy-coloured, iron-rich mineral) in sodalite.

The magical powers ascribed to sodalite are fewer than those for some other stones, but it is nevertheless said to be beneficial in several ways. Foremost of these attributes is a reputed ability to enable the mind to reach clear conclusions by combining intuition with logical thinking. It is also believed to encourage truth, to help express feelings and emotions, to calm the mind and to open the mind to new ideas and information.

Emotionally, sodalite is said to calm panic attacks, phobias, guilt and fears, and to give confidence to the insecure by enhancing their self-esteem.

In the realm of health, sodalite is thought to be useful in balancing the metabolism and cleansing the internal organs. It is also considered to be beneficial to the immune system and throat, to regulate blood pressure and to aid peaceful sleep. When several people gather together in the presence of sodalite, it is said to enhance their companionship and trust.

APPEARANCE AND COLOUR
Opaque mottled colours of pale to dark blue; more rarely, pink, lavender or yellow

AVAILABILITY IN BEAD FORM
Common

COUNTRIES OF ORIGIN
Brazil, France, Greenland, Myanmar, North America, Romania, Russia

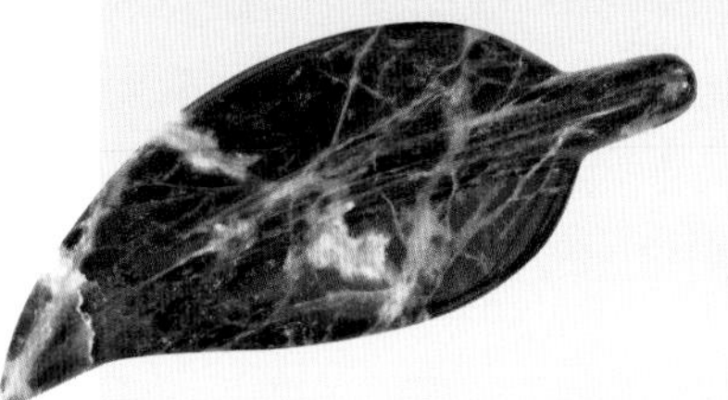

BUYER'S GUIDE

Sodalite is a common, inexpensive and colourful stone that is available in many sizes and shapes of bead. It is therefore very useful to those who are beginners to beading or who may want to make money from their hobby.

Blue Haze

Time to make 2 hours • **Ease of making** 4 • **Length** 61cm (24in), plus 14cm (5½in) drop

Just to show that findings need not always be used in the manner in which they were intended, this necklace uses bead caps in an unusual way. Normally, these are seen sitting immediately next to a large bead, fitting, as their name might suggest, like a cap. However, here they are used as links, because I could find no other that suited the purpose so well!

The carved sodalite flower is similar to others seen in the book, but as a variation it has two holes, making it suitable as either the centrepiece of a choker or, as here, part of a pendant drop.

The 3mm sodalite beads were a joy to use, very even in size and with good-sized holes for even threading. This is not always the case with semi-precious stone, and you should always check for variation in bead size before threading so that you can make allowance for any differences.

INGREDIENTS

- 1 carved sodalite flower with 2 holes, 40mm
- 3 x 40cm (16in) strings of sodalite beads, 3mm
- 2 silver-plated teardrop beads, 12 x 5mm
- 3 silver-plated fine tube beads, 6 x 1mm
- 10 silver-plated 4-holed bead caps, 9mm
- 13 silver-plated bead caps, 3mm
- 1 silver-plated 2-hole link
- 3 silver-plated small pendant drops
- 6 sterling silver crimp beads
- 1.5cm (⅝in) length of 'silver' gimp
- 2 x 8mm (⅜in) lengths of 'silver' gimp
- 2 x 71cm (28in) lengths of nylon-coated wire
- 40cm (16in) length of nylon-coated wire
- 20cm (8in) length of nylon-coated wire

TIP

When making tassels such as this, I usually make an odd number of uneven lengths, as I think it gives a more graceful appearance.

A

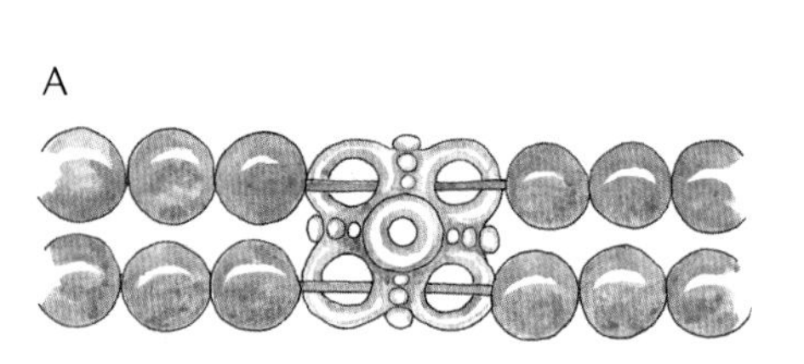

B

C

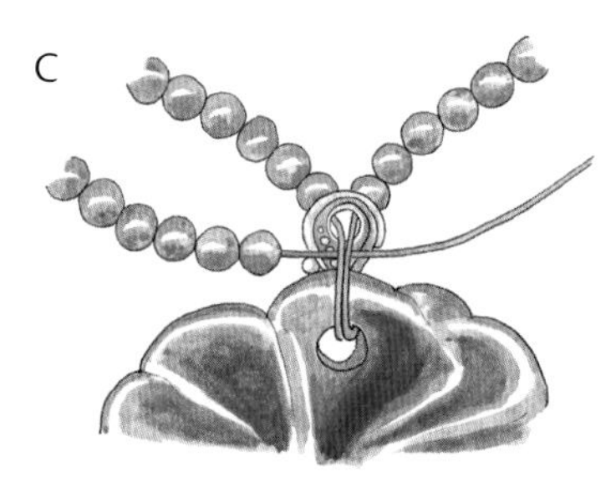

Rear view

1 Using one of the 8mm (⅜in) lengths of gimp and a crimp bead, attach the two long lengths of nylon-coated wire, treating them as one, to one part of the clasp (see Using Nylon-coated Wire with Gimp and Crimp Beads, page 15). Thread one of the silver-plated teardrop beads onto the two wires together, then thread 15 sodalite beads onto one wire and 16 sodalite beads onto the other wire. Now thread the two wires through the holes of a 4-holed bead cap, as in diagram A.

2 Thread onto each wire 15 sodalite beads and then another 4-holed bead cap. Repeat this sequence three more times.

3 Thread 9 sodalite beads onto the wire that in Step 1 was threaded with 15 sodalite beads, thread through one hole of the silver-plated link and through one hole of the sodalite flower from back to front, then through the other hole of the link. Thread on one sodalite bead and then pass the wire back through the hole in the link and the hole in the sodalite flower so that the single bead sits at the front of the link, as shown in the photograph. Then pass the wire back through the other hole of the link (diagrams B and C).

4 Thread nine beads onto this length of wire.

5 Thread 10 sodalite beads onto the other length of wire, then pass this wire between the link and the wires at the top/back of the sodalite flower (diagram B, rear view), before threading on 10 more sodalite beads.

6 Thread a 4-holed bead cap onto both wires and continue as in Steps 2 and 1 to match the first strung side of the necklace.

7 Thread the remaining length of gimp and a crimp bead onto the 40cm (16in) length of wire and slide to about the centre of the wire, then thread through the lower hole of the sodalite flower and back through the crimp bead to form a loop.

8 Do not secure the crimp bead, but instead pass one end of the remaining length of nylon-coated wire up through the crimp bead to hide its end beneath the gimp. After making sure that you have a neat loop with a fairly loose fit, secure the crimp bead by squeezing with your pliers.

9 Thread beads and the small bead caps onto each of the three lengths of wire, as shown in the photograph. Then, as if attaching to a clasp, use a crimp bead to attach a small pendant to the end of each wire (see Using Nylon-coated Wire with Crimp Beads, page 14).

Sodalite is found in large pieces and is inexpensive, and for these two reasons it is often used in carvings such as this elephant.

True Blue

Time to make 1 hour • **Ease of making** 3 • **Length** 21.5cm (8½in)

Sodalite is sometimes called 'the stone of truth,' so I wonder if that is where the 'true blue' saying originated? The 10mm beads used here are a very fine colour blue with almost no white veining, and they could quite easily be mistaken for lapis lazuli yet are a fraction of the price.

This is an easy item to make. Simply use the photograph as a guide to threading and follow the instructions for Using Nylon-coated Wire with Gimp and Crimp Beads, page 15. Note that although the spacer bars have holes, only the central and two outer holes are used.

INGREDIENTS

- 40cm (16in) string of sodalite beads, 10mm
- 6 blue large rocaille beads
- 21 gold-plated rondel beads, 6mm
- 6 gold-plated 5-hole spacer bars
- 2 gold-plated 3–1 end links
- 1 gold-plated toggle clasp
- 2 gold-plated jump rings
- 6 goldfill crimps
- 6 x 8mm (⅜in) lengths of 'gold' gimp
- 3 x 28cm (11in) lengths of nylon-coated wire

To reap the benefits of sodalite, it is said that you should wear or carry the stone for long periods of time.

Blues in Twos

Time to make 15 minutes • **Ease of making** 3 • **Length** 5cm (2in)

INGREDIENTS

- 2 sodalite beads, 10mm
- 8 blue very small rocaille beads
- 4 silver-plated fine tube beads, 6 x 1mm
- 4 silver-plated bead caps, 6mm
- 2 sterling silver beads, 2mm
- 2 blue anodized niobium coils
- 2 silver-plated headpins
- 1 pair of blue anodized niobium straight-leg ear-hooks

After making True Blue, four 10mm sodalite beads were left over, so I decided to make a pair of earrings with two of these. The design I chose is just about as simple as beaded earrings get, with the beads simply straight-threaded onto headpins and suspended from ear-hooks. Follow the instructions for Using Headpins, page 16.

Tiger Eye

The striking coat and glowing eye of one of our most beautiful big cats have given us the evocative name for the slightly stripy and silky ochre/brown version of this unusual decorative stone. All colours owe their silky lustre (chatoyancy) to asbestos fibres that, during the stone's formation, were replaced by cryptocrystalline quartz. The polished stone has a fibrous high sheen and has been prized as a protective talisman for centuries.

A great many attributes are ascribed to tiger eye and some of these relate to its reputation for having the power to bring together the energies of the sun and the earth. These 'down-to-earth' qualities are thought to create an increased awareness of the world and the needs of other people, to bring calmness and stability to troubled minds or situations, to aid practicality and wise decisions and to ensure a passion and energy for life as well as shelter in times of trouble.

Tiger eye is also reputed to bestow confidence, courage and beauty, create peacefulness, alleviate depression, assist creative talent and to aid intuition and insight. This latter attribute is said to be especially enhanced by taking a piece of the stone and holding it in the hand while gazing at it under the rays of the sun. By so doing, one is said to be able to see into the future.

Like many other stones, tiger eye is believed to be beneficial in treating, and protecting from, a variety of medical conditions, and the areas of the body thought to be so aided by this stone are the eyes, throat, reproductive organs, bones and muscles.

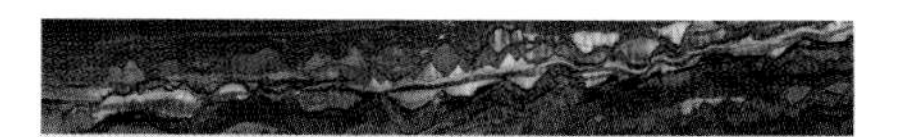

APPEARANCE AND COLOUR
Banded colours with a satiny lustre; brown, black, cream, yellow, blue and red

AVAILABILITY IN BEAD FORM
Common

COUNTRIES OF ORIGIN
Australia, India, Mexico, South Africa

BUYER'S GUIDE

Tiger eye is available in many sizes and shapes. The other colour versions are known by varying names, such as cat's eye (which is paler). It is inexpensive in bead form.

Burning Bright

Time to make 3 hours • **Ease of making** 4 • **Length** 71cm (28in), plus 10cm (4in) drop

This beautifully elaborate necklace is made from a mixture of tiger eye and matching-coloured rocaille beads. The large tiger eye beads are faceted – an enhancement that shows off the gorgeous rich colour and satiny sheen of this unusual stone.

This is an elaborate necklace that could also be made in other lengths and/or without the tassel to give a different appearance. This style, which incorporates so many rocaille beads, is a good money-saver, as only a few of the large feature beads are used and there are many left over from a 40cm (16in) string to use in other projects.

The magical powers of tiger eye are said to be enhanced when the stone is set in gold.

INGREDIENTS

- 9 faceted tiger eye beads, 14 x 10mm
- 58 tiger eye beads, 4mm
- 4 Swarovski crystal bicone beads, 5mm
- 22 Swarovski crystal bicone beads, 4mm
- 1 small packet of medium-sized rocaille beads in a toning colour
- 1 packet of small rocaille beads in a toning colour
- 17 gold-plated bead caps, 9mm
- 1 gold-plated cone-shaped bead cap, 9 x 8mm
- 6 gold-plated bead caps, 3mm
- 1 gold-plated rondel bead, 4mm
- 1 gold-plated toggle clasp
- 8 'gold' crimp beads (2 are hidden inside the calottes)
- 6 goldfill crimp beads
- 2 gold-plated clamshell calottes
- 3 x 56cm (22in) lengths of fine nylon-coated wire

Tiger eye has a reputation as a wealth-bringer, and the following little folk spell is supposed to bring in the cash! Take several pieces of the stone and 'impress' upon them your need for money, then lay them in a circle to surround a single green candle. Light the candle and wait for the money. If it works, please let me know!

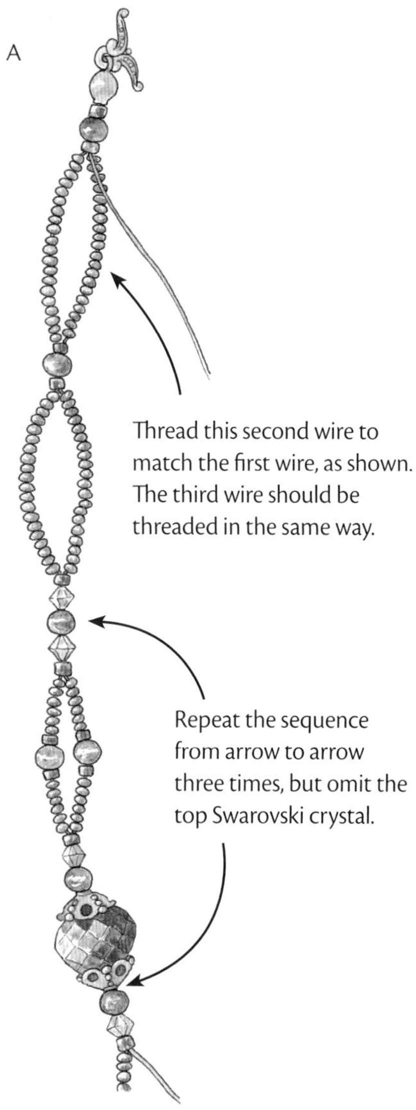

1 Secure a 'gold' crimp bead over one end of the three lengths of nylon-coated wire, then use a clamshell calotte to attach them to one part of the clasp (see Using Nylon-coated Wire with Crimp Beads and Clamshell Calottes, page 15).

2 Thread onto one of the wires the sequence of beads shown in diagram A. After the last large bead, thread on one more small bead sequence and then thread the large bead sequence shown in diagram B. Now thread on a 10–6cm (4–2½in) length of rocaille beads, which will form part of the tassel (made up of uneven beaded lengths). Apply a 'gold' crimp bead to the end of the wire as a temporary stopper.

3 Thread one of the other wires through the first three beads on the first wire. Then thread on 20 small rocaille beads and thread through the next medium rocaille bead and tiger eye sequence on the first wire. Thread on another 20 small rocaille beads, then thread through the next rocaille, crystal and tiger eye sequence on the first wire (diagram A).

4 Thread on six small rocaille beads, one medium rocaille bead, one 4mm tiger eye bead, one medium rocaille bead and six more small rocaille beads. Then thread through the rocaille, crystal, 4mm tiger eye, bead cap and large tiger eye sequence on the first wire (diagram A).

5 Repeat Step 4 three more times and then repeat the small bead sequence. Now thread through the central large bead sequence (diagram B) and finish, as with the first wire, by threading on a 10–6cm (4–2½in) length of small rocaille beads and apply a temporary crimp bead.

6 Repeat Steps 3–5 with the third wire on this side, and then repeat all the stages to make up the other side of the necklace.

7 When all threading is complete, adjust the beads on the lengths of wire to ensure that little wire is visible, but do not pull so tight that the necklace will not drape correctly. When you are happy with the appearance of the necklace, remove the temporary crimp beads, one at a time. After making sure that each length of the tassel is different to the others, thread on one medium rocaille bead, one crystal bead, one 4mm tiger eye and a 3mm bead cap, then apply a goldfill crimp bead close to the bead cap of each wire. Check that these are secure before trimming the spare wire.

A

Thread this second wire to match the first wire, as shown. The third wire should be threaded in the same way.

Repeat the sequence from arrow to arrow three times, but omit the top Swarovski crystal.

B

First wire

Second wire

All six wires have to pass through this final large bead sequence.

Thread on a 10–6cm (4–2½in) length of rocaille beads and then apply a temporary 'gold' crimp bead.

TIP

Before starting to thread, check that the holes of all beads at the lower centre of the necklace will take six thicknesses of thread, and if not, choose others that have large enough holes for this position.

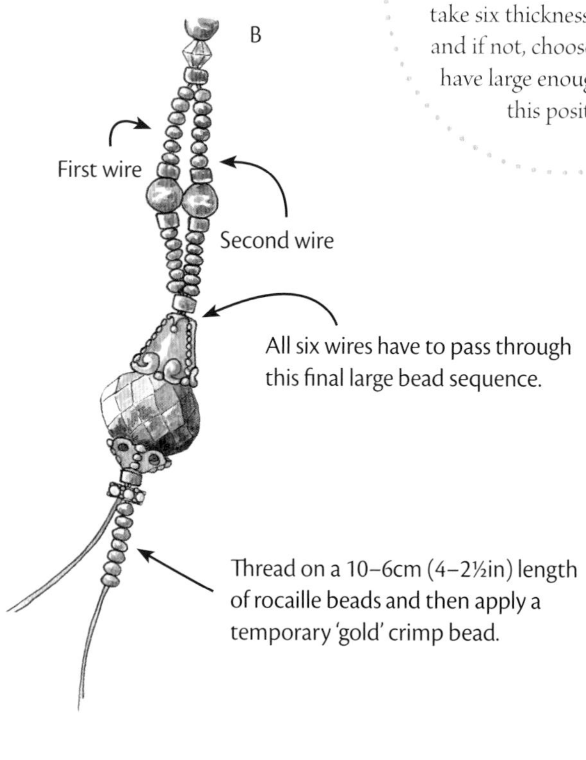

Most tiger eye occurs in shades of golden brown, but there are other colour variations, such as red and blue, and each of these has its own 'magical' attributes. Red tiger eye is considered to have stimulating properties, while blue has the opposite effect and is believed to bring calm to the over-anxious.

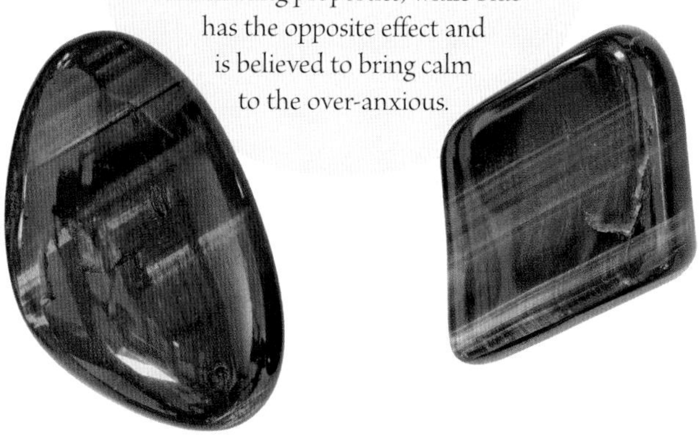

Burning Bright Earrings

Time to make 15 minutes • **Ease of making** 3 • **Length** 6cm (2½in)

INGREDIENTS

- 2 faceted tiger eye beads, 14 x 10mm
- 2 Swarovski crystal bicone beads, 6mm
- 2 goldfill beads, 2mm
- 2 gold-plated bead caps, 9mm
- 4 gold-plated bead caps, 3mm
- 4 goldfill crimp beads
- 2 x 8cm (3in) lengths of 'gold' nylon-coated wire
- 1 pair of goldfill ear-hooks

These earrings were designed to match the necklace, but make a beautiful jewellery item in their own right. They are suspended on 'gold' nylon-coated wire, which means that it is almost impossible for these earrings to be pulled apart and also gives them a lovely freedom of movement.

Simply use the photograph as a guide to threading and follow the instructions for Using Nylon-coated Wire with Crimp Beads, pages 14 and 17.

Autumn Fall

Time to make 40 minutes • **Ease of making** 3 • **Length** 53cm (21in), plus 5cm (2in) pendant

Reminiscent of autumn leaves, this necklace has, as its central feature, a tiger eye pendant that clearly displays the stripy nature of the stone. Other pendant shapes and sizes are easy to find in this stone type and could be suspended from a plain length of cord for a modern uncluttered look.

This is a good project for beginners to beading, as it is very simple and inexpensive to produce. To make this necklace, use the photograph as a guide to threading and follow the instructions for Using Nylon-coated Wire with Crimp Beads, page 14.

INGREDIENTS

- 1 tiger eye leaf pendant, 5cm (2in)
- 30 tiger eye beads, 4mm
- 40cm (16in) string of tiger eye beads, 3mm
- 4 goldfill heart pendants
- 10 gold-plated thin rondel beads, 4mm
- 18 gold-plated faceted bicone beads, 3mm
- 2 gold-plated bead caps, 5mm
- 1 gold-plated toggle clasp
- 4 'gold' jump rings
- 2 goldfill crimp beads
- 61cm (24in) length of nylon-coated wire

Tourmaline

The most common colour of stones in the tourmaline family is black, but it actually appears in a greater range of colours than any other gemstone. In its best form, these colours are clear and bright. In this respect, watermelon tourmaline is exceptional, as it displays many colours along the length of a single crystal. Some tourmaline changes colour when looked at in different lights, and most become electrically charged when heated or rubbed so that it will attract small particles of dust. It is a fairly hard but brittle stone that is found in small to very large crystals.

In general, tourmaline is widely respected as a gemstone with many 'magical' properties, among which are a reputation for invoking inspiration and self-confidence and an ability to point towards the truth or goodness of a matter. Tourmaline usually occurs in long wand shapes and it is these that are prized by those who use the power of stones. As a healing stone it is energizing and cleansing, and in many countries it has been employed by traditional shaman in the belief that the stone is able to confer powers of healing and protection on its owner.

In addition to the above, each colour of tourmaline has additional properties. For instance, pink crystals are reputed to banish emotional hurt and enhance love, while green tourmaline instils empathy, patience and joy in life; black tourmaline is protective against mobile phone radiation and encourages a positive nature; and yellow tourmaline enhances business dealings and is beneficial to those with abdominal complaints. A multi-coloured tourmaline crystal or a multi-coloured item of tourmaline jewellery is considered to combine all the qualities of each separate colour.

APPEARANCE AND COLOUR
Clear or translucent;
pink, green, blue/green, yellow, brown or black

AVAILABILITY IN BEAD FORM
Readily available, but not common

COUNTRIES OF ORIGIN
Afghanistan, Africa, Australia, Brazil, Italy, Pakistan, Sri Lanka, Switzerland, USA

BUYER'S GUIDE

Good tourmaline can be moderately expensive, but for those on a budget, tumble-chip beads such as these provide a good alternative and with a little imagination can be the main ingredient in beautiful jewellery.

Graduation

Time to make 9 hours
• Ease of making 9 **• Length** 51cm (20in), plus 3.5cm (1½in) drop

INGREDIENTS

- 1½ x 85cm (33½in) strings of mixed tourmaline tumble-chip beads
- rhodochrosite drop on bail, 30 x 20mm
- 1 gold-plated toggle clasp
- 2 gold-plated box calottes
- 2 gold-plated jump rings
- 2 x 50cm (20in) 'gold' medium (24-gauge) wire
- 1.5m (59in) length of black fine (28-gauge) wire

The name for this necklace sprang to mind for two reasons: firstly, and obviously, because it is a graduated style, and secondly, it is one of the more difficult items to make in this book, so those who successfully complete it could consider themselves graduated in beaded jewellery making!

The actual technique, however, is not hard to grasp or learn. It is just that the beads have very small holes and threading is tedious, and also that it is quite difficult to achieve an even circle of well-balanced beads. I had to unpick and go back many times before I was satisfied with the result.

However, I am sure that you will agree that the necklace is worth the effort, and who knows, it could be worthy of wearing to a graduation ball!

Tourmaline is reputed to be beneficial to plants and is even believed to be an insecticide, so maybe we should scatter some among our precious pot plants!

Many of the colours of tourmaline are combined within this necklace, so it could be considered to hold a combination of all the powers mentioned opposite for each.

1 Remove all the tourmaline tumble-chip beads from their strings and keep each colour in a separate shallow container.

2 Lay one set of ends of the two lengths of 'gold' wire side by side, then twist and bend to hold them firmly together (diagram A).

A

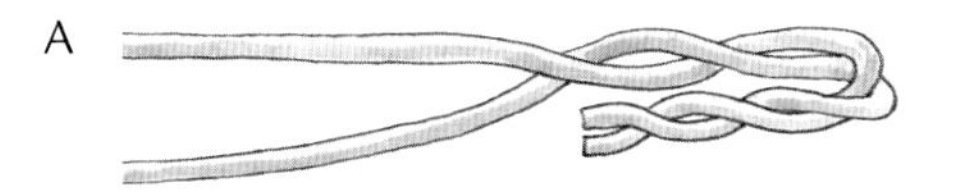

3 Thread on beads in graduated colours as shown in the photograph onto one length of the wire. I have chosen to start with black and have pink at the front, but you might choose another option. The length of this strand should be about 46cm (18in). Bend the threading end of this wire over to secure the beads while you work on the second strand.

4 Repeat Step 3 with the second strand of wire, but this time thread beads to a length of 48cm (19in), threading on the pendant drop in the centre. As you thread, make sure that each coloured section of beads is matching in length to those on the first strand. Take the two wires and, leaving about 4cm (1½in) of bare wire on each, twist the two wires together, as in Step 2.

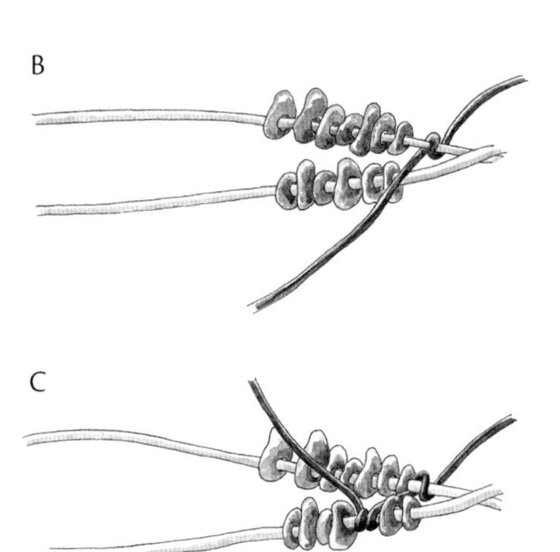

5 Wind one end of the length of black wire once around one of the two wires at the start of the beads already threaded (diagram B).

6 Thread one bead onto the black wire and take the wire diagonally across to the other length of 'gold' wire. Wrap the black wire once right around this length of 'gold' wire, making sure that it fits tightly between the beads (see detail above and diagram C).

7 Repeat Step 6 all the way round the necklace, remembering to match the diagonally threaded beads to the colour of those on the 'gold' wires nearby. However, as you progress, gradually increase the gap between the two 'gold' wires by threading on more beads at each diagonal. The number of beads threaded diagonally in the centre of the necklace should be about five or six, but this could vary according to their size.

8 When you have finished threading, check your necklace carefully and untwist the 'gold' wires to add or remove beads as necessary in order to make the wires on each side of the necklace of equal length. Then, at each end, twist the wires together, leaving about 1.5cm (⅝in) of bare wire. Trim the spare wire.

9 Use a strong pair of pliers to bend the ends of the wires over and apply a box calotte to each end of the necklace (see Using Thong or Cord with Box Calottes and Jump Rings, page 16). Finish off by using the jump rings to attach the clasp.

Lariat

Time to make 40 minutes • **Ease of making** 3 • **Length** 107cm (42in)

After the seemingly complicated previous project, I thought this necklace/belt would make a welcome contrast. The two large beads are tourmalinated prehnite, the tourmaline appearing as fine 'needles' of a darker colour.

To make the necklace, follow the instructions for Using Thong or Cord with Box Calottes and Jump Rings, page 16, to secure a box calotte to either end of the faux suede. Thread the rondel beads and the large beads onto two separate lengths of nylon-coated wire and use a crimp bead to make a loop at one end of the beads (see Using Nylon-coated Wire with Crimp Beads, page 14). Using a crimp bead, make a loop in the wire at the other end of the beads and attach to each of the two box calottes. The pendant drops and faceted bicone beads are threaded onto short lengths of nylon-coated wire, loops made with crimp beads (see diagram A, Using Nylon-coated Wire with Crimp Beads, page 17), then suspended from the loop below each of the large beads.

Prehnite is believed to bring unconditional love, intuition and harmony with the natural and spiritual world, while for health it is thought to alleviate problems of the urinary tract, chest and blood.

INGREDIENTS

- 2 flat tourmalinated prehnite beads, 35 x 25mm
- 4 silver-plated rondel beads, 4mm
- 8 silver-plated small pendant drops
- 8 silver-plated faceted bicone beads, 3mm
- 16 sterling silver crimp beads
- 2 silver-plated box calottes
- 1m (1yd) length of soft green faux suede
- 6 x 8cm (3in) lengths of nylon-coated wire.

Posy

Time to make 1½ hours • **Ease of making** 7 • **Size** 7.5 x 6cm (3 x 2½in)

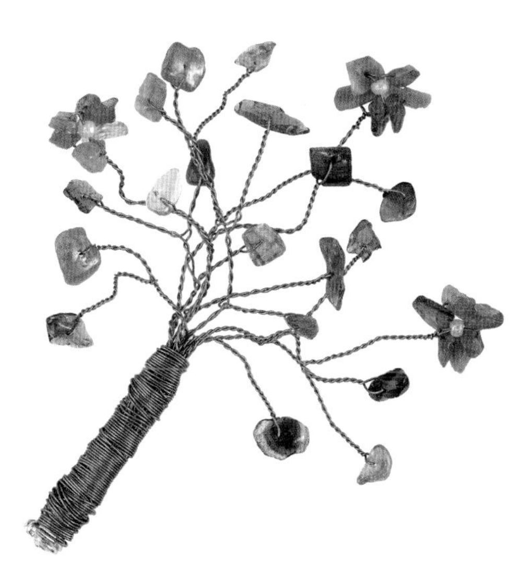

Posy is a delicate but fun brooch that could be made with almost any tumble-chip beads, but tourmaline lends itself particularly well to the design because of its varying colours – green for the leaves and pink for the flowers.

Maybe this would be a good project for a gift to a gardener friend, whose green fingers may benefit from ownership of tourmaline!

INGREDIENTS

- selection of green and pink tourmaline tumble-chip beads
- 3–4 creamy coloured small rocaille beads
- 1 metal brooch back
- 1.5m (59in) length of green fine (28-gauge) jewellery wire
- epoxy glue

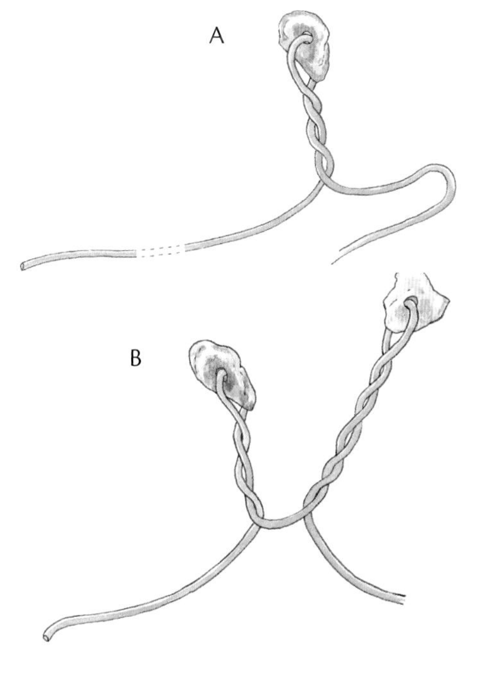

A slice through a pink tourmaline crystal from Pakistan.

1 Thread a single green tourmaline bead onto the length of jewellery wire and slide along about 12.5cm (5in). Bend the wire right over at this point, then grasp the bead and the wire between finger and thumb, and twist the wires together so that you have a length of about 1cm (⅜in) tightly twisted into a 'rope' (diagram A).

2 Thread on a pink bead, sliding it along to about 3cm (1in) from the end of the last twisted section, and bend the wire over. Then, as in Step 1, twist the two wires together so that the two twisted ends meet at the same point (see diagram B).

3 Twist the two wires together for a length of 7mm (¼in), then thread on another pink or green bead onto the long length of wire. Slide down the wire until it is about 1.5cm (⅝in) from the twisted wire, then bend the wire over and once more twist the wires together until you reach the remaining short length of wire. Twist this and the main length together for a length of about 1.5cm (⅝in). Leave a length of about 3cm (1¼ in) of untwisted wire, then bend the wire and bring the long length back up (diagram C).

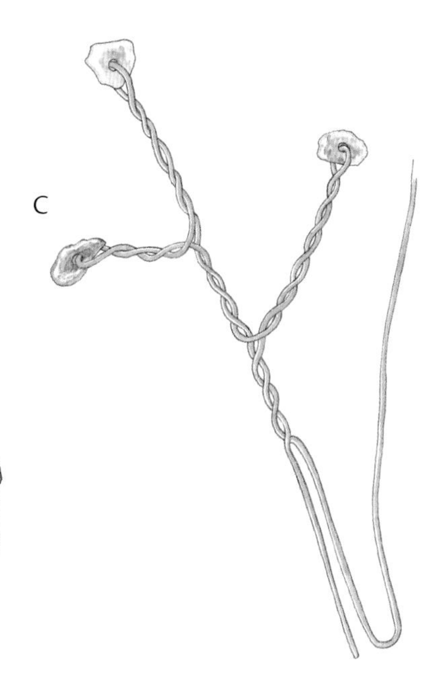

4 Repeat Steps 1–3 about seven times, or until you are satisfied with the appearance when all the beaded and twisted wires are bunched together, but vary the lengths of twisted wire and include a few single-stalked 'leaves' to give a more natural look. To make larger flowers, see diagram D for threading.

5 When you have finished threading beads and twisting wire, gather all the loose untwisted wire loops together (as if forming a bunch of flowers), then lay them along the length of the brooch back. Take the remaining length of unthreaded wire and carefully wind this around both the bunched wires and brooch back. Start at one end and cover all the wires neatly with a continuous tight coil of wire. When you are happy with the result, secure the end of the wire at the back of the brooch and then trim the spare wire. To make sure that there is no sharp wire protruding, cover the cut end with epoxy glue.

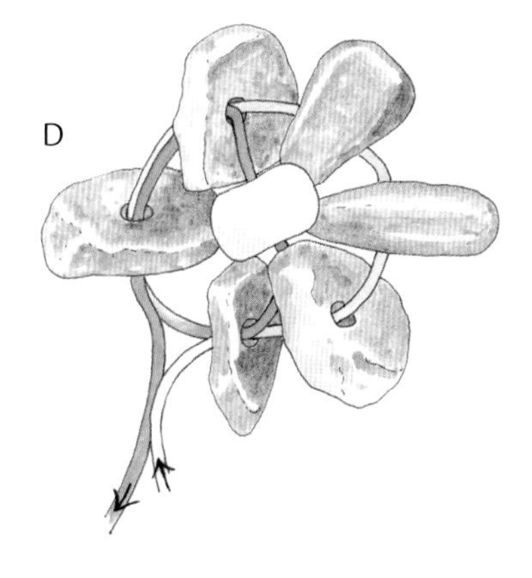

Turquoise

This beautiful opaque gem has long been regarded as a protective stone and a bringer of good fortune. It originates in aluminium-rich rocks, where weathering causes it to form crusts or fill cavities. 'Turquoise' is derived from 'pierre turquoise' – 'Turkish stone' – since Turkey was the main source in years past.

Turquoise is a soft, fragile stone that requires care in its handling. Very high temperatures can cause it to change to an unattractive green colour, and exposure to continuous sunlight, water or detergents and so on can cause it to fade to an extremely pale shade. Once the colour has been lost, it cannot be restored.

To many Native American tribes, turquoise was a sacred stone. The Navajo used it in rain-bringing rites and ground it to paste for sand paintings. Pueblos would lay a piece under their dwellings to ensure good fortune. Among the Apache, the stone was highly prized for its luck-bestowing qualities. Those who carried turquoise were believed to achieve a straighter arrow shot, while the unfortunate medicine man without the lucky stone in his possession was believed to have no power.

One of its most enduring attributes is a reputation for protection from falls, most commonly those from or by a horse. Turks would attach a piece of turquoise to the bridles or breast straps of their horses and a rider would also be sure to carry a turquoise amulet.

Even today, it is believed that a gift of turquoise will confer wealth and happiness on the recipient, while wearing the stone will bring new friends, increase beauty, promote marital happiness and ensure good health, especially in relation to eye problems, fevers and headaches.

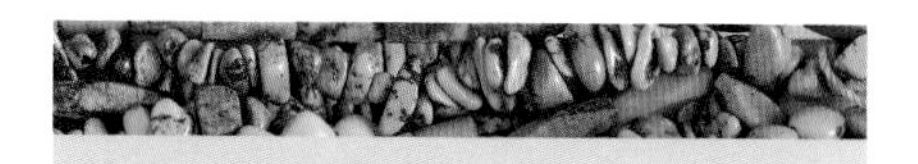

APPEARANCE AND COLOUR
Opaque shades of green, blue and turquoise, with black or brown veins

AVAILABILITY IN BEAD FORM
Relatively common, but often colour-enhanced

COUNTRIES OF ORIGIN
Afghanistan, China, Egypt, France, Iran, Mexico, Peru, Poland, Tibet, Turkey

BUYER'S GUIDE

Real natural turquoise is moderately priced and beads can be found in many forms, from simple rounds to unusual shapes, such as this Chinese rabbit. Imitation and colour-enhanced turquoise is in the cheaper price range.

Waterfall

Time to make 2 hours • **Ease of making** 3 • **Length** 58cm (23in)

The beautiful turquoise beads used in this necklace were made in China from stone mined in Iran. The colour is entirely natural and the surface of the stone is unpolished – a finish that I think suits the style of the piece. The size of the beads on both strings varies greatly, from 8 x 5mm to 15 x 5mm. The few accompanying beads and the clasp are silver-plated pewter.

Although this necklace looks expensive, the cost involved in making it is relatively low, but for anyone wishing to save money, colour-enhanced turquoise could be used instead.

TIP
Turquoise is a fragile stone that is easily broken, especially when it is in the form of small cut beads such as those used in this necklace. So take extra care during handling, and when storing the beads and finished jewellery.

INGREDIENTS

- 40cm (16in) string of turquoise tube beads
- 40cm (16in) string of turquoise rectangular beads
- 5 silver-plated fancy cube beads, 5mm
- 32 silver-plated hexagonal beads, 3mm
- 1 silver-plated 5-hole necklace spacer bar
- 1 silver-plated toggle clasp
- 15 'silver' small crimp beads
- 2 x 35cm (14in) lengths of nylon-coated wire
- 3 x 13cm (5in) lengths of nylon-coated wire

TIP
When using natural stone beads that are of irregular size, such as these, it is very important to lay the beads out in proposed order of threading prior to starting the necklace. This allows for adjustments to make both sides the same length. For this purpose, a beading tray is invaluable, as it holds the beads safely within its grooves.

1 Using a crimp bead, attach one end of one of the 35cm (14in) lengths of wire to one part of the toggle clasp (see Using Nylon-coated Wire with Crimp Beads, page 14).

2 Thread on the tube beads to form a length of 17cm (6¾in), then thread on a 3mm silver-plated hexagonal bead followed by a rectangular turquoise bead. Repeat the latter sequence twice, then thread on one more silver-plated hexagonal bead before passing the thread down through one of the outside holes of the 5-hole spacer bar.

3 Using the photograph on page 123 as a guide, continue threading the bead sequence as shown. After threading on the fancy cube bead, thread on a temporary crimp bead at the wire end and secure as before.

4 Repeat Steps 1–3 for the other side of the necklace.

5 Thread one of the 13cm (5in) lengths of wire through a crimp bead, slide the crimp bead to one end, then thread the wire almost completely back through again so that very little is visible on one side of the crimp bead (diagram A). Squeeze the crimp bead in place and trim any spare wire. Repeat with the two remaining short lengths of wire.

6 Thread each of the three short lengths of wire down through the remaining three holes of the spacer bar. Using the photograph as a guide, thread on beads in the sequence shown, finishing with a fancy cube bead. Apply a temporary crimp bead to each wire end.

7 Lay the necklace on a flat surface and gently push all the beads upwards so that they take up the slack in the wire. Check that each of the drops is of the correct length and then cut off the temporary crimp beads, one at a time, and apply a new crimp bead. If you are dexterous, finish these crimp beads off in the same way as in Step 5, but otherwise just trim the spare wire as close as possible to the crimp bead.

TIP
If you are looking for real turquoise, beware the very brightest or most evenly coloured stone, as this could be dyed or colour-enhanced.

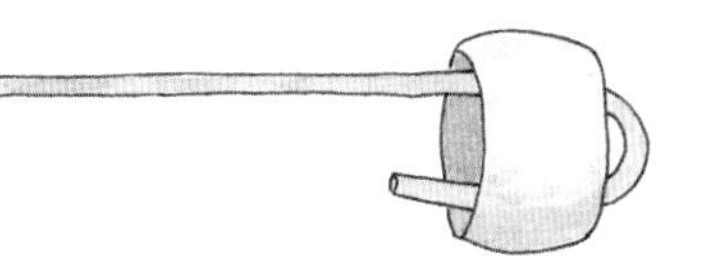

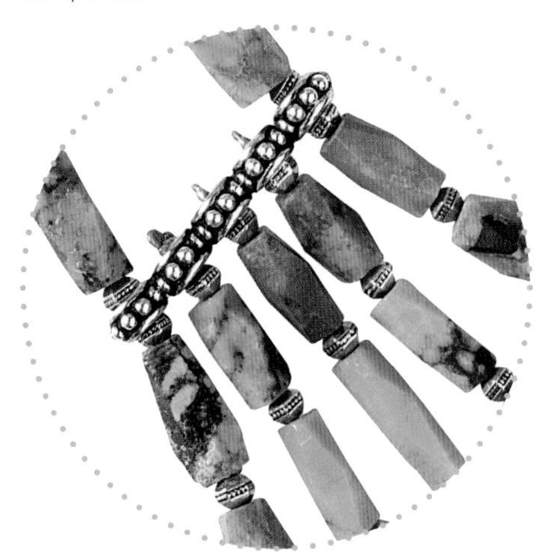

Circles Earrings

Time to make 15 minutes • **Ease of making** 3 • **Length** 5cm (2in)

These striking earrings complement the Circles Collar (opposite) and use up some of the leftover beads. They are simply made by using the photograph as a guide to the threading sequence and following the instructions for Using Nylon-coated Wire with Gimp and Crimp Beads, pages 15 and 17, to form a loop in nylon-coated wire and attach the loop to an ear-hook.

In Hindu legend, vast wealth comes to anyone who holds a turquoise in their hand while gazing at the moon on Pratipada night – the one after the first new moon. What a lovely thought!

Circles Collar

Time to make 3 hours • **Ease of making** 4 • **Length** 40cm (16in)

This exquisite little choker is made from a combination of beautiful square cushion-like turquoise beads, delicate AB-coated rocailles and small but perfectly formed silver-plated pewter beads. The stringing medium is fine nylon-coated wire, which provides enough spring to form the circular shapes and confer a stretchy flexibility that makes the necklace very comfortable to wear.

Beginners might look at this necklace and be daunted, but in fact it is very easy to make. It simply involves threading two lengths of wire that travel through the large turquoise beads in opposite directions. I have used 7mm cushion-shaped turquoise beads, but any other bead shape of approximately the same size will create a similar effect.

Looking for a suitable stone for a man? During the 17th century, turquoise was the height of English male fashion. A gentleman did not consider his attire to be complete unless he was wearing a turquoise ring! At this time, women scarcely wore the stone.

INGREDIENTS

- 40 turquoise beads from a 40cm (16in) string
- 1 packet of clear pale turquoise small AB-coated rocaille beads
- 39 silver-plated fancy rondel beads, 4mm
- 80 silver-plated thin rondel beads, 3mm
- 1 silver-plated toggle clasp
- 2 sterling silver crimp beads
- 2 x 8mm (⅜in) lengths of 'silver' gimp
- 2 x 80cm (31½in) lengths of fine nylon-coated wire

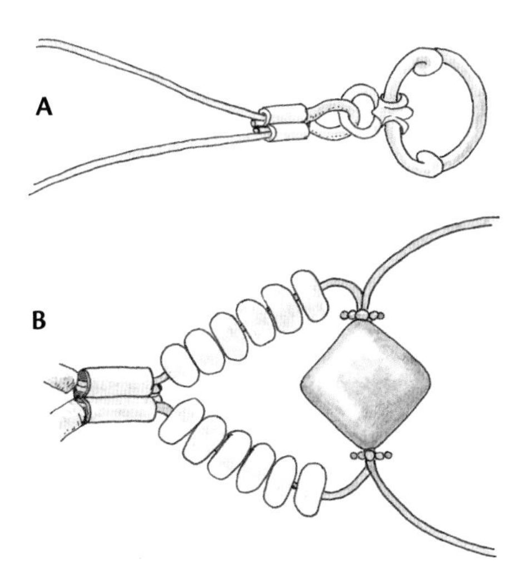

1 Using gimp and a crimp bead, attach the two lengths of wire together to one part of the clasp (see Using Nylon-coated Wire with Gimp and Crimp Beads, page 15). Trim the spare wire close to the crimp bead (diagram A).

2 Thread six rocaille beads onto each wire, then thread a 3mm rondel bead onto one wire, one turquoise bead and another 3mm rondel bead. Thread the other length of wire through the last three beads from the opposite direction (diagram B).

3 Thread onto one of the three wires six rocaille beads, a 3mm rondel bead, a turquoise bead and another 3mm rondel bead.

4 Thread onto the other wire three rocaille beads, a 4mm fancy rondel bead and three more rocaille beads. Thread this wire back up through the 3mm rondel bead, the turquoise bead and the 3mm rondel bead of the other beaded strand.

5 Making sure that the 4mm fancy rondel beads are all on the same side of the necklace, continue threading in the same way until you are satisfied with the length.

6 Complete the necklace by repeating Steps 1–2 in reverse order.

Glossary

AB-coating Short for aurora borealis, AB refers to a surface coating applied to some beads to give a special iridescent finish.
Bail Metal component to thread onto a necklace or cord from which to suspend a pendant.
Bead Caps Metal cup-shaped component of very variable size to fit close to and 'cup' a bead as part of the jewellery design.
Beading Tray Purpose-made tray with moulded necklace grooves to help with design, and also with depressed sections to hold beads while working.
Bicone Beads Beads that are cone-shaped at both ends.
Calotte, Box Square or rectangular metal component with side wings that fold over to hide the end of a length or lengths of thong or cord and secure it to the clasp.
Calotte, Clamshell Twin cup-shaped metal component usually used as a necklace end to hold and hide the end knot or bead of a necklace; it has a loop at one end for attaching to a clasp.
Crimp Bead A type of metal bead that is made to be squeezed with pliers so that it presses down onto a threading medium to secure it in place, often used together with nylon-coated wire to make attachments to clasps.
Ear-hook An ear-fitting that is worn by hooking through the ear.
Ear-stud or Ear-post An ear-fitting that has a straight 'post' that fits through the ear and is secured by a clutch-back.
Epoxy Glue A very strong two-part glue.
Feature or Focal Bead(s) The main beads in an item of jewellery.
Findings The general term given to all metal components used in jewellery making.
Frosted Glass A finish given to glass beads by tumbling in abrasive grits or by etching with acid.
Hatpin A long pointed pin (somewhat like a headpin) used for threading beads to make a decorative hatpin.
Headpin Metal pins (like small extremely fine, long nails) used for threading beads onto, for making earring and necklace drops.
Heishi Small metal tubes.
Gimp Very flexible open coils of extremely fine wire used for threading through and hiding the thread at the ends of necklaces.
Goldfill Metal finish of real gold bonded to a less-expensive metal.
Jump Rings Circles of wire used for joining one item to another.
Links/End Bars Metal bars with a single loop for attachment to a necklace clasp or ear-fitting on one side and multiple loops (2–5) on the other side, for the attachment of lengths of strung beads.
Memory Wire A hard, springy sort of wire that is made in continuous coils, from which lengths are cut to form the base of necklaces, jewellery and rings. It has the unusual property of returning to its original shape when pulled apart.
Nylon-coated Wire A type of wire that conceals multiple strands of wire beneath a smooth (often coloured), nylon surface. Extremely useful in beaded jewellery making.
Pliers Gripping and cutting tools used to assist with cutting and bending wire (see pages 12–13).
Rat-tail A silky-finish cord available in a large range of colours.
Rondel Bead Metal bead often used as a spacer between other beads, usually with relief decoration.
Spacer Bars Used in necklaces and earrings to separate the beaded strings in multi-stranded jewellery.
Superglue Cyanoacrylate glue in gel form, useful for sealing knots and other jewellery gluing jobs. Be careful not to get the glue on your beads, which will spoil them, or on yourself!
Teardrop Bead A pear-shaped bead.
Thread Conditioner Wax or silicone-type substance that can be applied lightly to beading threads to help protect them from damage when threading through small-holed or rough-edged beads.

Acknowledgments & Primary Suppliers

As always, thanks and love to my husband, David, who never fails to support my writing efforts by being a great first proof-reader and critic, and also for taking over the day-to-day household and gardening duties, leaving me free to work. And of course thanks to all my family, for whom I have less time than I should while I am writing. Thanks also to Vivienne Wells, editor and friend, who has the vision to see my proposed books in the way I do myself, and to guide them to fruition.

Most of the items in this book were supplied by the following companies:

Aquarius (France)
Tel: 00 33 251 647003
Email: keithbristow@wanadoo.fr
Wholesale suppliers of moldovite

Beaujangle (UK)
Tel: 01626 356322
www.beaujangle.co.uk
Suppliers of beads, findings and kits for all projects in this and my previous books

Burhouse Ltd (UK)
Tel: 01484 655675
www.burhouse.com
Wholesale suppliers of findings, and natural stone beads and other products

Dajeeti (UK)
Tel: 01227 372865
Suppliers of semi-precious stone beads

Fischen Minerals Ltd (UK)
Suppliers of beads and rough stone

Ilona Biggins (UK)
Tel: 01923 282998
ilonabiggins.co.uk
Suppliers of semi-precious stone beads

Lapidiary Shop (UK)
Tel: 01782 810914
Suppliers of polished stone

Mineral Warehouse (USA)
Tel: 01903 877037
www.minware.co.uk
Wholesale suppliers of all types of natural stone beads and other products

Reactive Metals Studio (USA)
Tel: 001 928 634 3434
www.reactivemetals.com
Manufacturers (wholesale only) of goldfill, sterling silver and niobium products

Tierracast (USA)
Tel: 001 503 678 2926 or 001 707 545 5787
www.tierracast.com
Manufacturers (wholesale only) of cast gold and silver-plated pewter

Other Suppliers

UK

Creative Beadcraft Ltd
Tel: 0044 1494 778818
www.creativebeadcraft.co.uk
Suppliers of beads, findings and storage, etc.

Earring Things
Tel: 0044 1513 564444 www.beadmaster.com

JRM Beads Ltd
Tel: 0044 2085 533240
www.beadworks.co.uk
Suppliers of beads, findings and storage, etc.

Kernowcraft Rocks & Gems Ltd
Tel: 0044 1872 573888 www.kernowcraft.com

Manchester Minerals
Tel: 0044 1614 805095 gemcraft@btconnect.com

The Rocking Rabbit Trading Company
Tel: 0044 8706 061588 www.rockingrabbit.co.uk

Spangles
www.spangles4beads.co.uk

USA

Bead Bar
Tel: 0014 074 268 826 www.beadbar.com

Beadworks
(various locations) Tel: 0023 038 529 108
www.beadworks.com

Bella Beads
Tel: 0015 036 352 073
www.bellabeads-shop.com

Buttons, Bangles and Beads
Tel: 0017 273 634 332
www.buttonsbanglesandbeads.com

Helby Import
Tel: 0017 329 695 300 www.helby.com
Wholesale only

Jewelex Collection
Tel: 0015 167 719 473 www.jewelex.com

Oriental Treasures Inc
Tel: 0016 156 465 383 www.look4beads.com

Shipwreck Beads
Tel: 0013 607 542 323 www.shipwreckbeads.com

WildAboutBeads.com
Tel: 0014 016 244 332 www.wildaboutbeads.com

Canada

Bead Closet
Tel: 0017 807 327 547 www.beadcloset.com

Beadworks
Tel: 0016 048 766 637 www.beadworks.com

Designer Beads
www.designerbeads.com

That Bead Lady
Tel: 0019 059 541 327 www.thatbeadlady.com

Germany

Gems 2 Behold
Tel: 0049 845 280 1667 www.gems2behold.com

France

Bead-e
Tel: 0033 450 914 034 www.bead-e.com

Le Comptor des Perles
Tel: 0033 130 870 808 kitou.serena@wanadoo.fr

Japan

Beadworks Japan
www.beadworks.jp

Australia

The Bead Company of Australia
(various locations) Tel: 0061 295 571 228
www.beadcompany.com.au

The Bead Shop
Tel: 0061 266 858 994 www.thebeadshop.com

Beadhouse and Casting
Tel: 0061 293 193 335 www.beadhouse.com.au

Beadzone
Tel: 0061 930 72811 www.beadzone.com.au

Crystal Flair
Tel: 0061 891 871 888 www.crystalflair.com.au

Ebeads Direct
Tel: 0061 410 399 445 www.ebeadsdirect.com

Not Just Beadz www.notjustbeadz.com.au

Spacetrader Beads
Tel: 0061 395 346 867 www.spacetrader.com.au

Unique Beads
www.uniquebeads.com.au

New Zealand

Beadz Unlimited
www.beadzunlimited.co.nz

Ebeads Direct
Tel: 0064 274 546 912 www.ebeadsdirect.com

Bibliography

The following books were used for reference:

The Curious Lore of Precious Stones
by George Frederick Kunz, published by Dover
Crystal, Gem and Metal Magic
by Scott Cunningham, published by Llewellyn
Love is in the Earth
by Melody, published by Earth Love
Rocks and Fossils
by Arthur Busbey 3rd, Roberts E Coenraads, Paul Willis and David Roots, published by Collins
The Crystal Bible
by Judy Hall, published by Godsfield
Crystal Awareness
by Catherine Bowman, published by Llewellyn

About the Author

Barbara's love of beads and beading began over 30 years ago with the gift of a rocaille bead necklace. From this small start, beads have led her on an interesting journey through manufacturing bead jewellery to supply of loose beads, and now to this, her third book. If you want to know more about Barbara, go to her business website www.rainbowdisks.com, and for any queries relating to the projects, email her at bd.thornton@onetel.net

Index